RAINBOWS
&
DRAGONS

ABOUT THE AUTHOR

BOB ROSS BEGAN SAILING AT the age of ten in the P-class trainer at the Plimmerton Boating Club on the shores of Cook Strait, New Zealand; he progressed to the two-handed Z-class then three-handed Idle Along.

After working in Wellington and New Plymouth as a journalist, Ross moved to Australia in 1955, aged 24 and worked on newspapers as a general reporter: Launceston Examiner (Tasmania), Daily Telegraph (Sydney) and finally the Sun News-Pictorial (Melbourne) from 1959.

At the Sun-Pic, in his spare time, he started a general boating column and began covering sailing. He went sailing again, on 21ft restricted class open boats, Lightweight Sharpies, Finns and keelboats on Port Phillip Bay and offshore.

Through Finns he met Colin Ryrie, the 1964 Olympic representative and 1964-65 Australian Finn class champion, who recruited him to be first editor of Modern Boating magazine, founded by Ryrie and business partner Jules Feldman, as the next magazine to Modern Motor in their growing Modern Magazines chain in Sydney.

After six years, Ross resigned and went freelance to become yachting correspondent for the Sydney Morning Herald and to write books.

With Ken McLachlan, business partner and advertising manager, he founded Australian Sailing, Australia's first all-sailing magazine, in 1976. He sold the magazine to the Yaffa Publishing Group of leisure magazines in 1986, and remained as editor until 2003.

RAINBOWS & DRAGONS

THE FORTUNATE LIFE OF YACHTSMAN
GORDON 'WINGNUT' INGATE

First published in 2019
Copyright 2019 © Bob Ross, Patrick Bollen
All rights reserved

Published by Boatswain Books • boatswainbooks.uk

ISBN: 978-1-912724-15-4

Designed and produced by Robert Deaves

All rights reserved. No part of this publication may be reproduced, stored in a retrieval system or transmitted in any form by any means, electronic, mechanical, photocopying, recording or otherwise without the prior written permission of the publisher, the author and any other copyright holders.

CONTENTS

Foreword by George W. Carmany III		7
Preface		9
Introduction: Personal Perspective by Patrick Bollen		11
1	Into racing, VJ and VS	27
2	Jasnar, Hobart race with a crew of youngsters	35
3	Building the house and a business	52
4	Dragons, first foray	62
5	5.5 Metres	72
6	Offshore with Caprice of Huon	96
7	Olympics in Tempest class	124
8	America's Cup campaign 1966-67	139
9	Gretel II 1977 America's Cup challenge	158
10	Gretel II, 1983 benchmarker Australia II 1983 America's Cup	177
11	New York YC and Royal Sydney YS cruises	195
12	Into farming	213
13	Back to the Dragons	217
The Awards		237

FOREWORD

I DOUBT THAT ANYONE WHO KNOWS Gordon Ingate has ever forgotten the first time they met him. I haven't. He's a force of nature.

My beautiful wife Judy and I moved to Sydney from New York in 1971 and, properly introduced to the Commodore, were presented with a guest card to the Royal Sydney Yacht Squadron. Soon afterwards we crossed the bridge to visit our prospective new club and strolled into the bar to have a drink.

In walked the dashing looking Gordon who extended his hand to me and announced his name in greeting, but, it did not escape my notice that his eyes were fixed on Judy. He has good taste. 'Come, why don't we sit over here and enjoy our drinks,' he said, which turned out to be his very diplomatic way of explaining that women at the time were not welcome in the Squadron bar.

Which is not to say that Gordon was awarded the Order of Australia Medal for diplomacy. I recall a press article years ago that referred to him as the 'mechant eleve' (naughty student) of Australian yachting. Let's just say that he was never known as shy, bashful, or unexcitable on the race course or, for that matter, ashore.

However, Gordon's contributions to Australian yachting are considerable; the Admiral's Cup; the Olympics; the America's Cup; my partner on something like 25 New York Yacht Club Cruises with many wins between us, and he's coming again this year (2018) at the spry age of 92.

He still competes in the Dragon Class world championship and notably has won the Prince Philip Cup Australian championship four times since his 80th birthday, including 2018 at 91. This is remarkable, and his collective record measured over time is one that no one can match.

Royal Sydney once circulated a questionnaire to the membership to ascertain their interests by day of the week. It is said that Gordon stood alone in checking the 'yacht racing' box for all seven days. His devotion to sailing is well-known, and it has made friends for him and for Australia around the world.

Gordon's a legend, although he would no doubt pass off that accolade as an acronym for 'ancient'. Bob Ross and I were friends during our Sydney days, now so long behind us, and I am sure yachtsmen everywhere will greatly enjoy his book about a true Australian 'original'.

George W. Carmany III
Boston. MA, June 2018

PREFACE

DURING 2017 AND 2018 I helped Gordon Ingate write his sailing biography after Gordon, at the age of 90, won the Prince Philip Cup Australian championship for the Dragon class for a third time in January 2017, capping an illustrious sailing career from childhood.

Ingate, nicknamed Wingnut years ago inspired by World War Two hero Major General Orde Charles Wingate, has since won the Prince Philip Cup for the fourth time in January 2018. His voyage includes wide international campaigning in Dragons, the 5.5 metre class, offshore racing and the America's Cup.

His Caprice of Huon won three of the four races in the 1965 Admiral's Cup in Australia's first appearance in the international offshore teams championship, then raced every second year from Cowes, UK.

In 5.5s, he won the Scandinavian Gold Cup at Hanko, Norway in 1969; and in 2001 not only won the 5.5m class at Kiel Week with My

Shout but was named overall Kiel Week champion for winning the most races in his class.

Ingate crewed by Rob Thornton, represented Australia in the Tempest class at the 1972 Olympics.

He campaigned for the 1977 America's Cup with Gretel II, which had been the strong challenger for the 1970 America's Cup under the ownership of Sir Frank Packer. She was narrowly beaten by Sweden's Sverige in the 1977 challenger elimination series.

Ingate continued campaigning Gretel II in Australia and was a valuable bench marker for the 1983 America's Cup winner Australia II.

He then returned to the Dragon class and besides contesting Australian events regularly spent the Australian winter campaigning in European waters in both the Dragon and 5.5 metre classes.

Ingate was always immersed in the socialising that went with sailing and so enjoyed competing in 30 New Yacht Club's annual cruises; port-hopping events along the east coast of the USA, with lots of partying after each leg.

Laughter is never far away when you are with Gordon Ingate. The attached picture, from his 90th birthday party, attended by 210 guests at the Royal Sydney Yacht Squadron, says much about the man.

Bob Ross

INTRODUCTION

PERSONAL PERSPECTIVE

by Patrick Bollen

BACK IN 1973 IT WAS more by good fortune than good management that I found myself living next door to one of Australian sailing's more notable characters.

He was a sailing champion, an ocean-racing conqueror, an Olympian and an America's Cup skipper. Gordon Wilson Ingate. In 2016 I visited his home.

Stepping into the living room waterfront home overlooking the calm and dark green aqua scape I am reminded of a yacht club trophy den with polished wooden cabinets full of gleaming silverware. From the lobby to the lounge the Ingate home is a shrine, a comfortable room lined with displays featuring a vast array of beautiful silver cups and ornate trophies, plaques, paintings, etchings, photographs and certificates of a lifetime's achievement's competing in sailboats on the bays, harbours, rivers, lakes and oceans of Australia and on the waterways of the world.

Gordon's grandfather Thomas Wilson Hodgson, Lord Mayor of North Sydney
INGATE FAMILY ARCHIVE

On the wall adjacent the fireplace is a fabulous oil painting by the late Jack Earl, of Gordon's magnificent Robert Clark design yacht, Caprice of Huon, sailing hard downwind to Hobart.

On March 29, 2016, Gordon celebrated his 90th birthday in the company of 220 of his friends, mates and family at his beloved Royal Sydney Yacht Squadron.

The guest list included many prominent names including Eileen ('Red') Bond, Sir James Hardy, John Longley from Perth, Ken and Barbara Beashel, former Olympian David Forbes, Gordon's brother Jack, a former Wing Commander in the RAAF, celebrated sailor Guido Belgiorno-Nettis, Bob Ross, John and brother Doug Sturrock and wives and many more.

It was a fabulous and joyous commemoration to a man who has achieved so much in his life and in his sport of sailing.

Youngsters Gordon (left) and Jack
INGATE FAMILY ARCHIVE

GORDON WAS BORN on March 29, 1926, in the Sydney suburb of Kingsford to parents Clyde and Greta Ingate.

Greta was the daughter of former Mayor of North Sydney, Thomas Wilson Hodgson, an architect who married Emily Muston. The Hodgsons were originally from Whitby in Yorkshire, the town that was home to the world's most prominent navigator, explorer, cartographer and scout, Captain James Cook.

Clyde's father came from Bath in Somerset in England. Clyde Ingate's family were in the jam business and also the manufacture of carriages. They once produced a carriage for the Royal Family.

Clyde Ingate was born and went to school in North Sydney. His name is on the honour board of the McMahon's Point high school. He served with distinction as an artilleryman in World Wars I and II. He won the Military Medal in World War I. "He got elevated to lieutenant because he was a good soldier and kept the gun firing while all his mates were being killed. He was badly injured and those injuries affected him until he died at the age of 67," said Gordon.

"He got wounded in the stomach; I understand shrapnel was found there when he died. His right arm was injured and withered over a period of time and he lost its use. The injuries he suffered in the World War I stopped him developing in later life and

Jack and Gordon 1930

Clyde and Greta Ingate on the day Clyde's regiment was shipped to Syria
INGATE FAMILY ARCHIVE

Gordon and his grandmother
INGATE FAMILY ARCHIVE

created the heart attack that he died from; comparatively young.

"When the Second World War came along, he put his age down where my brother put his age up to get into the Air Force. At this stage my father was a Lieutenant Colonel and he formed the Second Fifth Field Regiment and the Seventh Division.

"He thought, 'I don't need men; I need brains' so he went to Sydney University, spoke to the people in charge of the University Regiment, saying, 'I am here to form an artillery regiment and would like to interview guys who would like to join me.'

"My father's regiment, the Second Fifth Australian Field Regiment was the most decorated of any regiments in the war, the main recipient being Sir Roden Cutler, who got the VC."

It served initially in the Middle East in Syria, then Egypt.

Cubs Gordon (left) and Jack holding their dog Rajah / INGATE FAMILY ARCHIVE

The regiment was recalled to protect Australia and went to New Guinea. "Dad's regiment faced a major Japanese attack in Milne Bay, in 1943. Many were killed but earned a lot of medals. There is a book called Guns and Gunners that talks about my father starting the Second Fifth Field Regiment.

"The army kept him on. He became Commanding Officer of the Regimental Training Camp at Warwick Farm and was stationed there for four years training men in guns."

"My mother was born in North Sydney and her first home was at Number 3 West Street adjacent to St. Thomas' Anglican Church, which is today still serving the community.

The First Chatswood Sea Scouts
INGATE FAMILY ARCHIVE

"My brother Jack was three years older. We got on well together; growing up we were very close.

"My spare time was spent mostly building my railway set. I had a great Hornby train set and I also had a terrific Meccano set. Whenever I had any spare money, which wasn't often, I would race into town, into the city to buy more pieces for whatever construction programme I had underway at the time.

The Sea Scouts clubhouse
INGATE FAMILY ARCHIVE

"When I wasn't playing with my Meccano or Hornby train set, I was working at a big newspaper shop down on French Road in Willoughby, which ran off Willoughby Road. I also worked at the convenience shop on the corner of Sydney Road and Laurel Street in Chatswood. There I used to wrap butter and fill bags with sugar then I'd deliver these items on the owners' three-wheel box bike to homes in the district. It was fun and it gave me some pocket money.

Alice S with Gordon on the bowsprit. In the background, Kardos, the steel lifeboat
INGATE FAMILY ARCHIVE

This pocket money allowed me to buy Ibis, my first VJ.

"Jack and I began our schooling at Willoughby Primary before moving to Crow's Nest Technical School. I didn't like school much and I wasn't a good student. Jack was much better and he was a good sportsman. He loved his rugby.

"I still remember my first teacher Mrs Davies who lived in Sydney Road not far from my place. We used to walk home from school together and also Mr Ferguson who was a Stage 1 teacher in Grades 7, 8, 9 and 10. He used to call me garrulous Gordon and irrepressible Ingate and he took no hesitation using the cane.

"I was just nine years old when my brother Jack first took me sailing. It was the beginning of my long and successful sailing career."

GORDON JOINED THE Cub Unit of the Australian Scouting movement in 1935 at age of nine with the Chatswood Scouts, which had a Sea Scout division. Their rustic wooden boatshed was located on the water's edge of Sugarloaf Bay between the suburbs of Castlecrag and Northbridge. Five years later he joined the 6th Sydney Sea Scouts in Mosman Bay.

"I spent all my spare time at the boatshed. There was about 20 of us from all around the district and we'd spend just about all our waking moments from sunrise to sunset and sometimes beyond engaged in scouting operations and learning sailing, seamanship, splicing, knots, first aid, boat maintenance and the mundane chores like washing and drying up to cleaning the boatshed.

"At night we'd sit around telling stories. From Friday afternoon after school I'd head straight to the boatshed by bicycle and I wouldn't leave until Monday morning. We'd eat and sleep in the boatshed and I did most of the cooking.

"At the Sixth Sydney Sea Scouts Ellis Dash was the Scout Master. Ellis was just three years older than me, but I thought he was much older. At Chatswood we sailed a boat on Sugarloaf Bay called Alice S. Jack took delivery of Alice S and was the skipper.

Jack Ingate said: "Gordon was quite good at things he turned his hand to. He was not shy and he made friends easily. I was a patrol leader.

"Our community volunteer was a fellow named Mott, a retired Merchant Mariner on square riggers; a tough old seaman who had traversed many sea miles. Mott ran a very orderly boatshed.

Sixth Sydney Sea Scouts take the girls sailing on Petrel / INGATE FAMILY ARCHIVE

Gordon at De Havilland
INGATE FAMILY ARCHIVE

"We organised an old steel lifeboat, donated by P&O. We made a mast and a boom but it was such a heavy thing.

"When I joined the RAAF Gordon got the bug for sailing. The bug has manifested into a passion that has stayed with him the course of his very full life. I would've loved to continue my sailing but I was smitten by aeroplanes, particularly fighter aircraft."

While the two boys were out on the water almost every weekend, "Dad on the other hand spent most weekends in the army in the CMF, the Citizens Military Force. During the week Dad worked as a salesman selling canvas goods including sailcloth and carpets.

"Dad and Mum reasoned the best thing for me and Jack was to ship us off to scouts each weekend. They would look after us. I don't think they ever realised just how much Jack and I loved the sea scouts," said Gordon.

"My first attempt to get a job was when my father, through his business contacts, put me in touch with the general manager of the Sydney Water Board who did encourage me to study harder and to go onto university. However back in 1944 you couldn't get into university unless you attained a language pass at the Intermediate level.

"Because I didn't qualify with a language subject, I couldn't join the Water Board. I was really disappointed, however my father then managed to secure me a job at the De Havilland Aircraft Company where I worked in the drawing division of the engineering office.

"De Havilland had been commissioned to build the Mosquito fighter bomber, a wooden airplane designed in the United Kingdom and powered by two Rolls Royce 12-cylinder Merlin engines. The wooden parts were built in Sydney at the Beale Piano Company in Rozelle.

"My brother Jack flew one of these aircraft when he was on active duty in Europe. When his mission was complete, he attempted to return to England but crashed into a forest in Italy. Fortunately, he survived. Jack was always a pretty lucky bloke, He survived eight crashes in all. God knows how he did it," said Gordon.

Two hundred and twelve Mosquito fighters were built at Bankstown between 1943 and 1948. Some of these aircraft continued in service with the RAAF until 1953.

Jack Ingate was nineteen when he joined the RAAF and was based at Bradfield Park and later Temora before heading to Canada in 1942 to get his Wings.

So, while his younger brother was making a name for himself on the sea, "I was shipped off to England on a troopship along with 16,000 other officers and men to fight the bloody Germans on a Beaufighter," said 94-year-old Jack when I visited him at Huon Park, where he lived with his wife Rona.

Jack arrived back in Australia in 1945 after the war. He retired from the RAAF in 1971 and became a flying instructor with Australia's national carrier, Qantas. He continued to fly and perform aerobatics until 2016. He died in January 2019.

GORDON REMEMBERS BEING at De Havilland: "As a junior draftsman my job was to work with two older men who together taught me a great deal. One was Ted Kaufman who became one of Australia's great yachtsmen. He was an immigrant from Germany who reckoned he was a white Russian who got to Australia via China and Japan. The authorities thought Ted was a spy and so they kept him under close surveillance.

"The other bloke I worked with was Bill Waterhouse who became Australia's leading bookmaker. I was with De Havilland until I was 18 and then decided I wanted to join the Air Force but was not accepted into the military, as my job at De Havilland was deemed essential. "This was very upsetting. I thought I had a lot to offer the Force as I had a great knowledge of sailing. I was still in the Sea Scouts.

"I was still working with the aircraft manufacturer when the war ended, modifying engine controls. My boss at De Havilland was a chap named Miller who became a main partner in a business called Miller, Milson and Ferris. All of these men loved sailing so it was inevitable that I would get on well with them and later on, when I started in business, I did a great deal of work with them.

"After De Havilland I started a job as a junior builders' labourer at the Experimental Building Station of Australia. 'My father always maintained that we dress correctly. One morning in 1945 I dressed in brand new khaki overalls, a khaki shirt and khaki tie and boots, then rode my trusty pushbike from Willoughby to North Ryde to work. Reporting for duty they must've wondered just what hit them as I strode through the door. The bloke I answered to said, 'Come here son, I've got a job for you.' He led me down the workplace to the toilet block and showing me a badly blocked unit. So much for my brand-new attire."

To this day Gordon has no problems cleaning toilets, a skill so required if you become a boatie or a sailor. "There's a trick to cleaning toilets," says Gordon, "If you don't like the smell then breathe through your mouth."

Sally Saalfeld and her mother Nina at the Sirius Cove boatshed
INGATE FAMILY ARCHIVE

So, with the toilet now sparkling clean, Gordon later heard that the offending water chamber had been purposely blocked by a group of disgruntled employees who didn't believe they were being paid enough for the work they performed. "There was a very staunch union official among the workers.

Gordon was confident. "I had many beautiful girlfriends. One in particular was my first girlfriend, Barbara Johnson of Willoughby. Barbara was 16 and I was 17. Barbara was a wonderful young lady but she wanted to be married before she was 20. That wasn't going to work for me so I had to move on."

Founded by Gordon on the 1st October 1960, Rigby Jones was a metal processing company. Subsequently, Rigby Jones would eventually see him become a pioneer in metals fabrication. His first employees were Sam Rigby and John Jones and they became shareholders and directors.

What started as a small business grew into a large operation providing supply, cutting, forming, bending and rolling to fabricators, contractors, and project managers in the metal industry.

"From the Centrepoint Tower metal fabrication I was able to buy the Twelve Metre race yacht Gretel II from Alan Bond. The Domain Tunnel project enabled me to purchase my beautiful Caprice of Huon in which we represented Australia and competed in the Admiral's Cup in England in 1963 and the Overseas Shipping Terminal project in Circular Quay afforded my purchase of my Dragon Class yacht, Sea Fever."

ONE DAY HE met Sally Saalfeld, a vivacious, outgoing young lady from Mosman who shared Gordon's passion for sailing. She was a student at the Women's College within the University of Sydney, studying an Arts

Degree, majoring in Italian.

Sally was born in India where her father was a Colonel in the British Army. Colonel Albert Saalfeld was a classic old-school Englishman according to Gordon's lifelong friend and crewman, Bill Manning. "He was one of the last of the King's men.

"The Colonel was a fantastic man with a great sense of humour. Colonel Saalfeld would walk into head office of the CBA bank and go to the teller's chamber on the mezzanine level to deposit an envelope. He would say to the teller, 'Young man could you post this letter for me. Oh, and could you please ring the Imperial Services Club and ask if they would be good enough to page Colonel Saalfeld.' The Imperial Services Club was in Barrack street. When, leaving the bank, he arrived at the club as he was being paged. He had only just arrived in Australia and thought this was a good way to be introduced."

Sally and Gordon's wedding
INGATE FAMILY ARCHIVE

Sally grew up in England until the outbreak of World War II when she migrated to Australia with her family. She attended and completed her schooling at the Frensham Girls College in Mittagong.

Albert, his wife Nina and the family moved to Mosman and into a federation house with a boatshed on the shores of Sirius Cove facing east on Sydney Harbour. The Colonel kept a VJ there for Sally who persuaded her mother to crew for her and together they entered many races representing the Mosman VJ and VS Club. Sally was one of the first female members of the club.

Sally raced a VJ in partnership with her mother and for three years together they won the Mosman Sailing Club Championship. They also

Siblings Stephen and Christine
INGATE FAMILY ARCHIVE

became the Double Bay VJ champions.

Sally went off to a meeting one evening at the Mosman Amateur Sailing Club. There she wondered who the talkative young man on the other side of the clubhouse was. This was when Gordon met Sally, the beginning of a wonderful relationship. They married in 1951.

GORDON HELPED ARTHUR W. Byrne on his way to his fortune when Byrne approached him asking if Gordon could, 'Form some sheet metal,' so he could produce a garage door. Nothing was too difficult for Gordon who said he could and so the answer to easy opening and closing garage doors, invented by an Egyptian employed by Arthur Byrne, was born.

Arthur then asked if Gordon could roll fabrications for ten doors, which soon became ten thousand. Gordon told Byrne that, "If you want ten thousand then you'd better go off and set up your own factory." The rest is history.

Their friendship endured the many decades that followed competing in the sport of ocean racing and their shared interest in the business of manufacturing. Byrne passed away in 2009 at the age of 86.

Gordon, Sally and Stephen Ingate at Stephen's graduation / INGATE FAMILY ARCHIVE

Gordon set about building his house in Cammeray on Sydney's lower North Shore. A simple three storey construction on the water's edge overlooking the tree enshrouded landscape that was Northbridge Golf Course. When it came to putting a roof on his home, he researched a better way of achieving a flat roof construction. Approaching the bank manager for a loan he was confronted with the question, "What do you propose to put on the roof?" Gordon replied, "Malthoid." [Black tar and paper]. "Not on our roof," said the bank manager. "You'll put on copper."

Not convinced, Gordon who, when at De Havilland, worked with an engineer who suggested that a new product called aluminium was as good as copper, would do the job and so Ingate put an aluminium roof on his new Cammeray construction thus becoming the first flat residential aluminium roof in Australia. The roof, has today, well and truly stood the test of time.

At this time, he and wife Sally entered into parenthood with the birth of two children, a son, Stephen and a daughter, Christine. Stephen was born on 12 January 1956 and Christine on 16 December 1958.

They both have fond memories of a life with Gordon however, "Dad was always so busy with work and when the business didn't consume his time he was always sailing," says Stephen. "I started my schooling at Brierley Street Kindergarten, Neutral Bay public school and finally at The King's School at Parramatta where I was a boarder. When I was in my first year at King's during an assembly the head of Prep school, the Reverend John Price, announced a headline from one of Sydney's leading newspapers, 'Ingate, Champion of the World.'

"I was nonplussed but later was very proud of Dad," says Stephen.

Stephen did take up sailing but not to the same extent as Gordon. When he graduated from The King's School Stephen went off to Sydney University to study Arts and Law. While at University he lived on campus at St Paul's College.

Stephen's third son John, says of his grandfather, "Skip is hectic, stressed, passionate, determined and tenacious," while number four son Chris, echoing his older brother's sentiments adds, "Skip is effervescent, charming, driven and generous."

Stephen's sons regale in many stories about their grandfather and all reflect their great pride in him and his many triumphs. Stephen's eldest, Nick, thinks Gordon's recipe for success is a motto for life, "Commit to the task, one task at a time and be determined."

Tony Hearder, close family friend, neighbour and son of Ingate's later partner in life, Margaret Hearder, recalls his first ocean race. "It was a Friday afternoon and I was playing on the street just up the road from where I lived, on Cammeray Road on my scooter or bike when Gordon drives up beside me honking the car horn.

"'Hey Tony,' he said. 'What are you doing tonight?' 'I don't know,' said Tony. 'Look, I'm a bit short of crew tonight, do you want to come sailing?' said Gordon.

"'Um Okay, but I'll have to go and ask Mum,' said a young Tony Hearder.

"So off I go sailing with Gordon Ingate. It was a Bird Island Race and that was my initiation to ocean racing. I still help him out today if he is short of crew and you know, nothing changes. He is still a gruff, demanding, boisterous and commanding skipper. He knows what he wants and he wants to win," says a laughing Hearder, 45 years since he first sailed with Ingate.

Stephen Ingate recalls his younger days discovering sailing with his famous Dad as he was gaining some notoriety. "I do remember doing a Sydney to Pittwater sail with Dad on a 5.5 metre keelboat called Kirribilli and for safety reasons I was tied in. My early days of sailing were interesting to say, the least," says Stephen, who agrees that he probably sees more of Gordon today than when he was growing up.

"We spent many wonderful summers aboard Caprice of Huon when we'd cruise to Pittwater with the Hearders. It was Christine who inherited Dad's sailing ability and determination," says Stephen.

Christine Ingate was educated at Sydney Church of England Girls School (SCEGS) Redlands at Neutral Bay on the lower North Shore. She also attended Sydney University and The Women's College and studied economics.

"Christine was good. She could mix it with the best and often did against the likes of Olympic sailors Iain Murray, Gary Gietz, Neville Whitty, to mention a few," says Stephen Ingate.

"Dad is a flat-water sailor. Christine is like dad. She inherited his power of concentration and his focus. When Chrissie and I were little kids Dad did the Brisbane to Gladstone race only because he could get Caprice to the Whitsunday Islands. What a family holiday that was sailing to South Molle and Long Island and cruising the beautiful Whitsunday Passage. We were lucky children.

"Then Dad took Caprice to Bowen, a little fishing town on the North Queensland coast. While there Gordon had the engine serviced. One night while serving dinner Sally noticed water rising over the cabin floor. Soon over her ankles the water was flooding quite rapidly. Dad pulled the engine compartment apart and revealed that the service engineer had overlooked the reconnection of a hull fitting and water was pouring in. We were sinking. Dad, with little fuss, calmly and quickly remedied the problem. We pumped the bilge dry, cleaned up the cabin floor and soon all returned to normal. There were some pretty harsh words dished out to the serviceman the next morning, as you can imagine."

Sally's younger sister, Ally, believes Gordon's success was not one based on luck. "Gordon is a charming and adventurous man. I don't think it was luck, as I believe he created his fortune. By that I mean he surrounded himself with good people. Gordon was a delegator."

Ally was also born for the water. "I was five years younger than Sally. My beautiful sister always looked after me but it was Gordon who taught me how to sail. Like Sally, I was also the club champion one year at the Mosman Amateur Sailing Club. I wouldn't have been if it hadn't been for Gordon and Sally."

Gordon and John Hearder's friendship was founded on their great love of sailing, a friendship that endured and together, along with their families they enjoyed many wonderful adventures and cruises.

Dorothy Cora Louise Sally Ingate passed away on April 1, 1998.

His mate John Hearder and wife Margaret were a great comfort to Gordon in difficult times.

"They got on well just as they did when Sally was alive," recalls Tony Hearder. "We spent so many great times together and one in particular was a cruise we did to the Whitsundays. We were just kids then and we all boarded Caprice of Huon and set sail on the trip of a lifetime, eight of us aboard Gordon's magnificent yacht. We four kids, Stephen and I and my sister Susie and Christine were the crew. The parents helmed and navigated and cooked.

"We'd drop anchor in some beautiful, protected bay and would be in the dinghy even before the anchor settled into the bottom and off we'd go to explore the beach or an island. We had so much fun.

"Back on board, Margaret would prepare dinner. We'd sit together around the saloon table and in the cockpit before settling in for a game of cards. Sally loved playing cards and Stephen and Chrissie also became quite adept at pontoon.

"My mother was a great cook and a wonderful hostess. She loved entertaining," said Tony. John Hearder passed away two years after Sally Ingate in 2000. Before he died, he asked Gordon should anything happen to him, would he look after Margaret. Well, as fortune would have it and as they were such good friends Gordon and the beautiful Margaret Hearder did become partners and enjoyed a wonderful life together until Margaret's peaceful demise at her home at Pearl Beach on April 22, 2015.

"Gordon and Mum were terrific together. She had a wonderful life with both my father and Gordon," says Tony. "Gordon is great bloke. He is a charming man who still has a keen eye to beauty. He is a persuasive and driven man, a high achiever as is seen by his yachting prowess and success not only on the harbour but nationally and internationally," said Tony Hearder.

And so, at 92 years of age, Gordon Wilson Ingate, an icon of Australian yachting and sailing still showed up each Saturday morning in the summer season with a grin on his face and an enthusiastic greeting for everyone who engaged him as he strode confidently down the dock at the Royal Sydney Yacht Squadron to join his long-time crew member, David Giles ahead of yet another battle upon the harbour.

As if his trophy rooms could do with any more silverware. And may another rainbow pop out of his arse.

1

INTO RACING, VJ AND VS

GORDON INGATE FIRST WENT SAILING at the age of nine on Sugarloaf Bay, Middle Harbour, with the First Chatswood Sea Scouts on a 16ft skiff called Alice S, so named with the S acknowledging the Shipway family who had donated the boat to the scouts. His 12-year-old brother Jack, who was a patrol leader with the scouts, was the skipper.

Sometimes they carried tents and camping equipment to sleep overnight on long cruises around Sydney Harbour. "One weekend we sailed this boat from Sugarloaf Bay, down under the Spit Bridge, around Middle Head, up under the Harbour Bridge, under the Fig Tree bridge to the weir at the head of the Lane Cove River. If we couldn't sail, we would row."

Ingate began sailing competitively at the age of 14 after he had moved to the Sixth Sydney Sea Scouts on Mosman Bay, firstly in a Vee Jay and then its successor, the Vee Ess; two popular Australian skiff designs of the 1930s and 1940s.

Gordon steering his first VJ Ibis, with Beryl Mulgannon
INGATE FAMILY ARCHIVE

They were designed by Charles Sparrow, a draftsman at Sydney's Cockatoo Island dockyard, who in the 1930s occasionally sailed on the open 12ft skiffs with Sil Rohu, who owned a gun shop on Castlereagh Street in the city and lived on the waterfront at Vaucluse.

Rohu saw the need for a safe and exciting easily-sailed small boat that could be built at home, perhaps by a boy and his father, manned by a skipper and crew that was unsinkable and could be righted after a capsize without outside help.

He encouraged Sparrow to design an 11ft 6in skiff with its planked hull completely decked in except for a small well big enough for two pairs of boy's feet with extra body hiking leverage extended by two sliding planks.

The first boat, Splinter, was built by members of the newly-formed Vaucluse Amateur Sailing Club and thoroughly tested before final drawings were made. The first boat built to the modified plans was Chum, launched in 1931 and a class quickly formed, despite Australia being caught in a financial depression.

Sparrow recalled, "Complete details were furnished with each set of plans sold, together with a list of materials covering every single piece of material in the boat including fastenings and fittings. At that time the completed boat was expected to cost five pounds 17 shillings and sixpence and the sails about three pounds five shillings. I donated the plans and the specifications to the Vaucluse Junior Amateur Sailing Club for their use, with any revenue earned to go to the club's future development of the class.

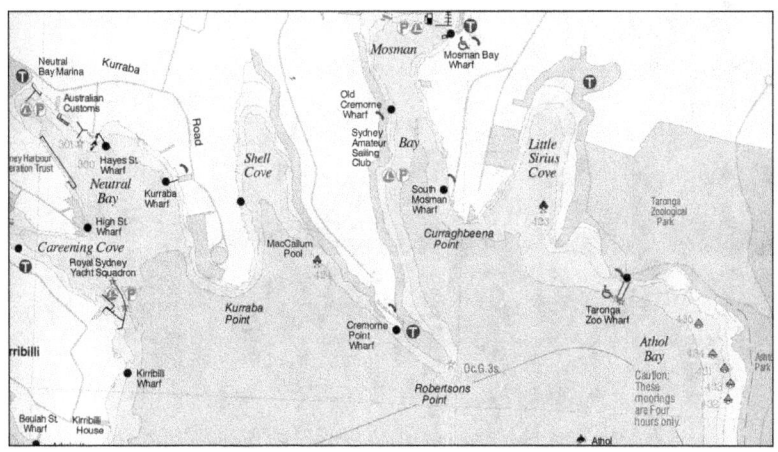

Mosman Bay and Sirius Cove / NSW ROADS AND MARITIME SERVICES

"We had hoped that boys, once they reached the age of 18, would go on to sailing the larger open boats that were so popular on the harbour in all sorts of sizes. We eventually found that this wasn't happening so, in 1936, I designed an adult version of the Vee Jay. This was known as the Vee Ess or Vaucluse Senior. She was designed upon the same lines as the Vee Jay but was 3ft 6in longer and had a cockpit that was big enough to allow two lads to sleep in it using the sail over the boom to make a tent."

The three-handed Vee Ess quickly caught on and was still racing as a class in 2019.

Gordon Ingate bought a Vee Jay called Ibis from his earnings as a paper boy for seven pounds and on the long delivery sail from Gladesville to Sugarloaf Bay on Middle Harbour found that it leaked very badly. Becoming dissatisfied with the Scoutmaster at the First Chatswood Sea Scouts, he moved to the Sixth Sydney Sea Scouts at Mosman Bay on Sydney Harbour. "Every weekend I spent all my spare time at the boatshed until I was 19. I took my Vee Jay down there and learned to sail the hard way.

"I used to ride my push bike down there after school on Friday and stay there until Monday morning. We would go sailing with people looking for crew, like Peter Luke and Harry Newton Scott; with members of the Sydney Amateur Sailing Club and the Cruising Yacht Club of Australia including Jack Earl and his Kathleen Gillett. We were useful because we were light and nimble to go up masts.

"We learned a lot about sailing by having the shed in Mosman Bay

Vee Ess fleet at Max's boatshed / INGATE FAMILY ARCHIVE

because we were right in the midst of things."

He raced with the North Shore Vee Ess and Vee Jay Sailing Club which came into being in the early years of World War II when five Vee Esses – P.G. Taylor, A.H. Cobby, Smithy, Aroha and Whispering – got together and started to race. The first three boats were owned by George Mills, the club's popular president, and named after famous wartime pilots. "George Mills was a pilot wounded in the First World War who strongly believed that sailing had a very real role to play for developing pilots in the Second World War, giving them an appreciation of the wind's behaviour," said Ingate.

FOUR MORE BOATS followed. Mills arranged space to house them in the Cremorne Boatshed, owned by Max Emcken and known as Max's, on the present premises of the Sydney Amateur Sailing Club. By 1948 more than 20 boats were racing regularly with the North Shore Vee Ess and Vee Jay Sailing Club, which had moved to a new clubhouse to the north in Mosman Bay 100 metres from the Mosman Rowing Club.

Ingate, at the age of 16, in 1942 decided to build himself a Vee Ess with the help of his uncle, Cliff Hodgson, who was a carpenter and taught him the use of tools.

He called it Barracuda. "I launched the boat where the Middle Harbour Yacht Club is at the moment, sailed it around to Mosman Bay, went sailing the next Saturday and along came a southerly buster. I wasn't experienced enough; the boat tipped over, washed up on Robertson Point and completely broke up; a brand-new Vee Ess, which wasn't very pleasant," said Ingate.

"I then went about building a new boat called Sea Fever. I didn't need any help from my uncle at this stage; I had learned enough about it. Dad got a bit upset because we had to move his car out of the garage to build it."

Ingate built Sea Fever with spruce frames left over from De Havilland's wartime bomber construction project and the first sheets of waterproof plywood. "That's when I met Ted Kaufman who built a Star in spruce. We used to visit the scrap heap in Stanmore at a piano factory that De Havilland took over during the war. "And I built a triangular mast out of this beautiful spruce."

Gordon with Sea Fever
INGATE FAMILY ARCHIVE

By then Ingate had become secretary of the club, which had changed its name to the Mosman Amateur Sailing Club, where he met his wife to be, Sally Saalfeld and her mother who had an old Vee Jay and offered to help them. "Cliff Gale, a senior member of the Mosman sailing community, also put in some time helping them rig their boat, improving their boat and they became successful enough to buy a champion Vee Jay from Pittwater and with that boat won the Double Bay championship."

Ingate kept Sea Fever at the Saalfeld's boatshed at Sirius Cove and became socially involved with them. "I was invited to stay with them over weekends and had my own special room."

THE 1947-48 SEASON opened on Saturday October 4 with a general handicap race in which 15 boats competed. During the season boats from the club took travelled to events at Newcastle, Taree, Ballina and Pittwater. Over the New Year period Sea Fever, with Ingate crewed by John Nippard and Geoff Ruggles, won the New South Wales championship on the Manning River at Taree, with Geoff Thorne's Wendy from Vaucluse second.

Six selected boats from the North Shore club contested the Australian championship on Sydney Harbour in February. The Vaucluse club carried off all the prizes although the North Shore club was not among the

Sea Fever at Neutral Bay Hacienda
INGATE FAMILY ARCHIVE

also-rans and Sea Fever was consistently in the first six placings.

In a report for the April 1948 edition of Australian Power Boat and Yachting magazine, Ingate wrote: "A subtle difference between the older and the younger club is that the latter appreciates that sailing can be at times a dull affair without the company of the fair sex and the lady membership of the North Shore club does much to foster the spirit of both social and sailing activities of the many lady members sailing in crews.

"An active season is planned for next year as many members are building and acquiring new boats and it is estimated that something like 50 boats – approximately 30 Esses and 20 Jays – will go to the starting line. To have achieved so much without the great advantage of having a clubhouse has been a grand effort but it is realised that it is essential to obtain club premises if the North Shore club is to retain and strengthen the keenness of this sporting fraternity. Our committee is at present actively engaged in endeavouring to find property or the necessary finances with which to build suitable premises.

"There are 28 clubs sailing Vee Jays and Vee Esses in the Commonwealth of Australia affiliated with the association. First constituted as an Australia-wide organisation in 1937, the Vee Ess and Vee Jay offers to all sailing organisations the means of training an ever-growing number of young lads who will later take their place as keen and efficient members of the crews of large yachts and the North Shore Club is doing its part in

Sally with her VJ and mentor Cliff Gale
INGATE FAMILY ARCHIVE

popularising this splendid sport."

Sea Fever finished third in the 1948-49 Australian championship at Sandringham YC on Port Phillip. The winner was Yandoo, skippered by John ("Chocko") Winning from the Vaucluse club with 385 points from Othello (N.Little, Victoria) 301 and Sea Fever 265.6.

Sea Fever on the road to Taree where she won the NSW championship
INGATE FAMILY ARCHIVE

The following season, on Sydney Harbour, Sea Fever was fourth in the Australian championship behind Winning's Yandoo, a new Vaucluse boat Avenger 2, skippered by Peter Cole, who was to become one of Australia's leading sailmakers and yacht designers, and Geoff Thorne's Wendy.

Ingate's career in Vee Esses then came to an end when he began skippering the Saalfeld's offshore racer Jasnar in 1950.

His Vee Ess sailing paused in 1947 when he won trials conducted by Royal Sydney Yacht Squadron on Sydney Harbour to represent Australia in the singlehanded 12ft Firefly class at the 1948 London Olympics in a fleet including Colin Ryrie and Roger Gale. But his boss at the

Sea Fever, 1946–47 season
INGATE FAMILY ARCHIVE

Sea Fever
INGATE FAMILY ARCHIVE

Commonwealth Experimental Building Station would not give him the time off to go. "The team travelled by ship, six weeks to go from Sydney to England."

Victorian Bob French, eventually gained selection and finished 18th in the fleet of 21; understandable as he had never seen a Firefly. "The Australian trials were sailed in the 14ft Island class boats which usually had a crew and to sail them singlehanded was a helluva handful."

GORDON'S VS WAS named after John Masefield's classic poem Sea Fever [*I must down to the seas again, to the lonely sea and the sky, And all I ask is a tall ship and a star to steer her by...*]and carried the symbol JM (Masefield's initials) surrounded by a circle with two wings on her mainsail and the crew's clothing.

Masefield's work was significant for Gordon because right from his earliest days he liked the water, undimmed by an early escape from drowning in the Georges River at Casula on a sea scouts outing. "We cooked lunch and all had something to eat when some of the boys went in swimming earlier than they should have. One of them went under and panicked," said Ingate.

"He was probably 12 and I think I was 14. I tried to calm him down but he grabbed me by the neck, I passed out and to my mind I had drowned. Thank heavens, the scout master dived in and saved us both. I can remember being brought to by the scoutmaster laying me on a warm, flat rock and pumping me out. To my mind I was dead.

"Ever since that time I have never been afraid of drowning; it was a pleasant, warm feeling. That helped me not being worried about being on the water."

2

JASNAR, HOBART RACE WITH A CREW OF YOUNGSTERS

THREE MONTHS AFTER CELEBRATING HIS 90th birthday with a vibrantly entertaining lunch for 210 guests at the Royal Sydney Yacht Squadron on March 29, 2016, Gordon Ingate gave himself a birthday present. He purchased the 69-year-old double-ended 29ft sloop Jasnar, which, as a 24-year-old, he had skippered in the 1950 Sydney-Hobart race with a young crew that included his wife-to-be Sally Saalfeld.

With that special sentimental attachment, he had followed Jasnar's history through various owners until one day when he was driving across the Spit Bridge he recognised her, moored on the northwest side carrying a for sale notice. After lengthy negotiation he bought the boat from Tony Morrison of Seaforth and on June 3, 2016, had her delivered to the pontoon berth he has right below his harbour cliff-side house in Cammeray.

"What are your plans for the boat," I asked, as we watched a delivery crew berthing her. "To look at it," Ingate said.

"Sail it at times?"

Jasnar practising for the 1950 Sydney–Hobart / INGATE FAMILY ARCHIVE

"Possibly. I lead a pretty busy lifestyle and at 90 years of age I have got to figure out a way of being able to get on board the boat from the pontoon because I am not quite as active as I used to be. I bought it for purely sentimental reasons, because it would deteriorate unless it was looked after. I will restore it and look after it and decide whether to give it to a museum or give it to the Sea Scouts."

Jasnar was designed by Wally Ward and built in 1947 for Ken Patrick of Mosman, of the Patrick Shipping Company family, who named her Tern. Ward designed her to the metacentric shelf principle, which serves as a guide to achieving equal buoyancy in the dissimilar ends of a design to achieve balance and so reduce weather helm.

Ward, an amateur designer later, in collaboration with boatbuilder Ron Swanson who designed the sail plan with favourable rating in mind, designed the 30ft Carmen class. One of them, Cadence (Jim Mason) won the Sydney-Hobart race in 1966.

Colonel Albert Saalfeld, who had served with the British Army in India and through World War Two was an intelligence agent, moved to Australia with his family from the UK in 1946 to a waterfront home on the northern side of Sirius Cove, Mosman. He had been a member of the Royal Thames Yacht Club and done some sailing in England. He bought Tern in 1948 and re-named her Jasnar.

She was not named, as some believed, after an Indian dancing lady. Jasnar was an acronym for the Christian names of the family: J (John Saalfeld, the colonel's son), Allene (daughter), Sally (daughter), Nina (mother), Albert (the colonel) and Rose (his mother-in-law).

Ingate had got to know the Saalfeld family through VJ and Vee Ess racing at the Mosman Amateur Sailing club where Sally and her mother had a VJ and through keeping his Vee Ess Sea Fever at their boatshed in Sirius Cove at times.

They invited him to sail occasionally aboard Jasnar, cruising as a family on Sunday and in Sydney Amateur Sailing Club harbour events and Cruising Yacht Club of Australia short offshore return races to Coogee, Kiama and Bird Island.

Ingate already had some offshore experience from his time in the Mosman Sea Scouts whose youngsters were always in demand as fill-in crew on ocean racers moored in Mosman Bay including Peter Luke's Wayfarer and Jack Earl's Kathleen, which both sailed in the first Sydney-Hobart race in 1945, and New Silver Gull, Harry and Oceana Newton-Scott's wishbone ketch.

Sally Ingate and Jasnar in Sirius Cove / INGATE FAMILY ARCHIVE

He soon learned that he was prone to seasickness. "I first went on Wayfarer, one Friday night start, to go around Lion Island and back to Sydney. A lousy southerly was blowing and boy was I seasick. I kept sailing on Wayfarer, did a Bird Island race on her; very slow because Peter didn't have the money to buy new sails and the boat was a bit off colour. He lived on it at Mosman Wharf."

The Jasnar crew became so proficient offshore as well as inshore that Ingate asked Colonel Saalfeld if he could take her in an ocean race to Bird Island and back. "'Yes' said the Colonel, 'Do you think my wife would like to go, with Sally?' and they came as crew. Sally was excellent, Cookie (Nina) got seasick and for some unknown reason I wasn't sick on that trip," said Ingate.

"We did very well. We went in a few more offshore races and I started to talk to Wally Ward about the rating because she had never been measured for ocean racing and he said she should rate very well under RORC. And we talked about how to improve her performance. The Colonel was happy to go with old sails but once Cookie got aboard and started to like it she put some money into the boat and sails."

They extended the mast, to take a bigger mainsail and carry a jib topsail and a masthead genoa that was used more like an asymmetrical spinnaker for better light weather performance.

With the rating improved, Ingate asked Colonel Saalfeld if he could take Jasnar in the Sydney-Hobart race. "To my surprise he said: 'Yes, but only if you take Sally as part of the crew.' She had proven to be a very good sailor and I was only too happy to take her. She was engaged to a young medical student, John McLeod. I wasn't interested in any situation with Sally. I knew she was a good helmsperson from sailing on the VJ and she knew enough about sailing on Jasnar to fit in very well."

Ingate put together a crew with an average age of 22: Keith Tierney, Bruce Jackson, Keith Wells, Gary Mailer and Sally, who was 21, a third-year arts student at Sydney University, who also served as the cook.

Removing the engine was on the race preparation list. In those days

Sydney-Hobart yachts did not need to be equipped with an auxiliary and Jasnar's was a very old light petrol engine converted from a 1930's Rugby motor car. "I thought it would help the rating," explained Ingate.

Ingate appointed Keith Wells as navigator. He was 21, doing an apprenticeship as a seaman that included a course in navigation. On Boxing Day morning as they went down the steps of the Saalfeld home to Sirius Cove, where Jasnar was moored, Ingate asked: "Are you under control with the navigation?"

"He said, 'No trouble, I've got all here in the book.'

"What book?

"'This is all the stuff on navigation that I need.'

"It was a school atlas."

"'Don't worry Gordon, It's all under control. All you do is go out through the heads, we turn right and I'll tell you when to turn right again.'"

The fleet of 16 started on Boxing Day in a southerly gale that blew for two and a-half days and raised rough seas. Jasnar, the

Above: The mast was extended to take a jib topsail. Below: Jasnar shows her double-ended lines
INGATE FAMILY ARCHIVE

Loading stores on Christmas Day
INGATE FAMILY ARCHIVE

Preparing Jasnar on Christmas Day afternoon, from left: Keith Tierney, Gordon Ingate, Gary Mailer / INGATE FAMILY ARCHIVE

Jasnar crew on Boxing Day morning, from left: Keith Tierney, Gordon Ingate, Sally Saalfeld, Bruce Jackson, Keith Wells, Gary Mailer / INGATE FAMILY ARCHIVE

smallest boat in the fleet, from a good start in Sydney Harbour and under a storm spinnaker, was well placed at the Cap Heads.

"We went around South Head and holy shit the seas were big. We were reefed down, we had a small jib on and in no time, I was seasick; Jesus I was crook," said Ingate.

"Ellida, Jack Halliday's 34ft sloop, hit a wave that shook the toilet off its mount. They went back to the harbour and started 24 hours later. Mistral II (65ft schooner), the biggest yacht in the fleet, blew out a jib and ran off in a north-easterly direction to help the crew retrieve it. "I said, 'Guys, we are in front of a 65-footer.'"

Jasnar set off on a south-east course at a speed of approximately four and a-half knots, her log recorded: "Rough to very rough seas, short high swell, overcast and dull. Shipping spray overall and occasionally a short sea for'ard. Vessel working and leaking around mast and stays; pumping at regular intervals."

At 2300, with the wind south force 7 (28-33 knots), Jasnar tacked onto a new course, southwest by south, "very rough seas, short high swell, overcast, shipping spray overall", said the log entry.

During the morning of the 27th the southerly eased to moderate and shifted southeast in the afternoon. Through the 28th the log recorded at noon: "Moderating seas and swell – fine, clear weather". Jasnar was abeam of Montagu Island at 14.30, on course in a 7-10 knot east-southeaster. At 1900, when she could see the loom of the Green Cape lighthouse, she set a parachute spinnaker.

Jasnar fully powered. Note the canvas dodger / INGATE FAMILY ARCHIVE

Meantime, at the head of the fleet Margaret Rintoul, Austin Edwards' 44ft yawl skippered by 1949 winner Merv Davey, had led the fleet into Bass Strait by 12 miles from Mistral V a 47ft Sparkman and Stephens designed sloop skippered by Jock Muir for Guy Rex of Hobart, as the wind fell light on December 28, shifted south and then north-east.

Through December 29, the wind freshened to 30-40 knots from the north-east, for a fast ride across Bass Strait. Jasnar, down to her number two main and number one spinnaker was in bother as the nor'-easter freshened to 28-33 knots. The log records: "12.15 vessel broached uncontrollably, spinnaker pole broke and port runner track carried away. Steered SSE until repairs effected and storm spinnaker set. 15.30 resumed S course. Speed approx seven and a-half knots. Vessel estimated to be surfing at 14-15 knots on wave crests."

While the runner was re-secured by a block and tackle, Ingate had to go aloft in a makeshift harness to re-insert the starboard crosstree, which was shaking out of its socket. "I was able to put the bolt back in, it had not come out totally, to resecure the crosstree," he said.

Jasnar off the New South Wales coast
INGATE FAMILY ARCHIVE

Aloft, Ingate was in danger of falling out of the harness when the boat heeled to a wave, swinging him out and back into a cap shroud. "The wire caught me right between the balls; it hurt like hell. 'I'd better not pass out, I thought, or I will fall out of the harness.'"

During the evening, Jasnar's log recorded 30 miles covered in three hours and at 11pm: "Full gale blowing from NE – very rough high seas and shore swell."

Margaret Rintoul, the race leader, off St Patrick's Head at 8.30am on December 30 was hit by a southerly change at up to 50 knots. All day long the yachts plugged into the howling southerly. Colin Haselgrove's 45ft Nerida from South Australia, in third place, snugged down to double-reefed main and working staysail, was slow and uncomfortable against the big seas. As the passage between Schouten Island and the Freycinet Peninsula appeared to leeward, Haselgrove decided to run through it into the calmer waters of Oyster Bay.

That night Nerida, under large light-weather headsails, held a direct course for Tasman light as the wind hauled towards the west. At dawn, off the Hippolyte Rocks, she was only a mile behind Mistral V, which had been more than 25 miles ahead. But when the wind died there, Mistral V left Nerida wallowing in the left-over slop. Margaret Rintoul, which had spent the whole night offshore tacking into the remnants of the blow, appeared from out to sea to round Tasman Island close astern of Mistral V.

Margaret Rintoul was first to finish, at 16.15 on New Year's Eve, under spinnaker on a freshening sea breeze, 18 minutes ahead of Mistral V. Nerida won on corrected time by 3hr 9min from Margaret Rintoul with Mistral V third.

Meantime, back aboard Jasnar, Keith Tierney had become seasick, as well as Ingate, in the first southerly blow, leaving three men and Sally to sail the boat. Besides cooking, Sally cared for the seasick sufferers. "Boy I was dry reaching," said Ingate. "I thought I was going to die."

Then he discovered a cure: "A great way of getting over seasickness I found in the early stages of that race and I understand it works for other people; when you finish vomiting you feel good for a couple of seconds or maybe a minute or so. Have a glass of water; drink it straight away; that stops you from dry reaching.

"And when you stop, the best thing to get back into your innards what you've lost is rich fruit cake. It's got sugar; it's not dry or hard to swallow. Then when you're sick again, up she comes; it's just in and out. More water, more fruitcake. Do it three times and you're not seasick any more. Fortunately, we had a few fruitcakes on board. We had to throw all 20 loaves of our bread overboard. It was specially baked by David Jones. At lunchtime on the first day it all went green with mould; they had put too much preservative in it."

Sally nursed Ingate through his seasickness, which eased as the southerly shifted southeast and then east for Jasnar off Jervis Bay. "We had a lovely trip across Bass Strait then a second southerly hit,

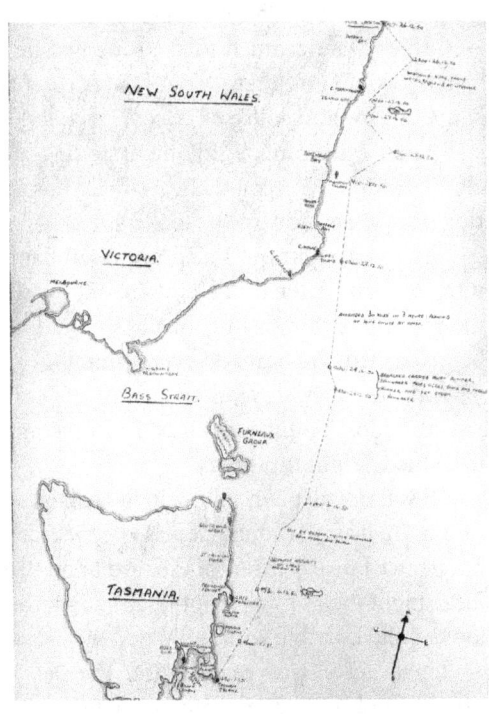

Jasnar's track: 'Turn right and right again'
INGATE FAMILY ARCHIVE

but I wasn't seasick through it," said Ingate.

In an article she wrote afterwards for the Sunday Sun about her experiences in the race, Sally said: "Seven days of being battered, bumped, jolted by the incessant movement of a yacht at sea, of being cooped up without privacy with five men, of being always being too busy or too tired to think, does not sound much fun. But I want to do it again. Anyway, you are alternately too busy and too exhausted to care much about anything except the time your boat is making.

"Part of my problem solved itself – I didn't even change my clothes for the first five days. I started out with tons of spare clothes, but the first night out the bilge water got into my locker. Not that that mattered much – I was always so busy I just didn't seem to getting around to changing.

"I didn't wear any makeup either. I must have looked pretty ghastly. In fact, once or twice our skipper Gordon Ingate, ordered me to comb my hair.

"I think I put lipstick on only twice in the whole race and when I did, it made me feel a different person.

"There was so much to do, time just flew. Before the boys went on watch I would give them scrambled eggs, spaghetti, baked beans, rice or soup, or stew and coffee or cocoa.

"And I had so much tidying up to do – people would keep throwing clothes around. I seemed always to be hanging up wet clothing, or putting dry things away in the lockers.

"The first night out I slept on a sail bag, with water dripping down into my hair. After that I crawled into a sleeping bag on a bunk. But there was one thing all my business could not keep me from noticing – being bashed and bumped every time I took a step. First, I was bumped against the galley stove, then against the companionway into the cabin. I'm sure I lost pounds this way. I can recommend it to any girl wanting to reduce weight in a hurry.

"It was not all plain sailing in the galley either. The bread got a kind of fungus on it and I thought it was all my fault. It made me very depressed. Then once I nearly threw out for'ard hand Bruce Jackson's false tooth. He just caught me as I was emptying it down the sink in a mug of water. He looks quite horrible without it too."

Ingate recalls in preparing for the race taking the labels off all the tinned food, in accord with seamanship best practice of the time, so that they would not wash off and jam the bilge pumps. "But we forgot to write the contents on them. So, we would sit down and Sally would say,

'Shall I open this tin?' We never knew what we were getting. Sometimes it was peaches when we were expecting Irish stew."

The second southerly gale hit Jasnar at 1600 on December 30 but eased that evening to a very light southerly by midnight. As the leaders finished on New Year's Eve, Jasnar was 15 miles east of Wineglass Bay, just making steerage way in a four-knot easterly, 40n miles north of Tasman Island. Keith Wells' "I'll tell you when to turn right again" navigation to Hobart had continued to worry Ingate. Wells had taken sights under difficulty through the two southerly blows. "I'd say to Keith, 'Where the hell are we?' And he would say, 'She's thar' and put his thumb over the whole of Australia on the atlas."

"Eventually we gybed when Keith said we could lay Tasman Island and there right in front of us was the gap between Tasman Island and Cape Pillar, the south-eastern corner of the Tasmanian mainland. I should have pulled away but I said, 'What are our chances of going through there?'

"Keith said, 'I've had a look at it on the charts and it's very deep water, yeah we can go through.' I think he had worked out that the current was favourable and the four-knot breeze was definitely going to take us through."

In his log entry, Wells recorded: "12.30: passed through Tasman Island Passage with five-knot set, vessel estimated to be moving at

The gap between Tasman Island and the mainland / STEFANO GATTINI (ROLEX)

approximately 5-10 knots with parachute spinnaker; 1000ft cliffs each side, channel approximately 250ft wide. New course W x S to lay Cape Raoul."

THE SYDNEY-HOBART RACE sailing instructions were subsequently re-written to prevent its yachts taking the short-cut, which saved Jasnar many miles. "It was pretty awesome," said Ingate. "We got through very quickly, became becalmed under the Hippolytes had a nor'easter going across Storm Bay for a beautiful sail to the Iron Pot where, of course, there was nothing.

"It still upsets me to think we are arriving from an ocean race and the last 15 miles is in a bloody river with no wind and the tide against you. "I can remember sitting there with a piece of marlin attached to the headsail, it was so frustrating after I had this feeling we had done quite well, having saved a lot of miles, going through the Tasman peninsula gap. We got there about nine o'clock at night and didn't finish until 3.15am and I always feel for the people caught in that dilemma of arriving at the Iron Pot and finding the last 11 miles that bad. It was bloody awful."

Sally, with the distinction of being the second woman to finish a Sydney-Hobart race, behind Jane Tate, who sailed in the second running of the race in 1946 with her husband Horrie aboard Active, had a different perspective, recorded in a personal scrapbook under the heading "The Most Wonderful Day of my Life":

"Thursday, January 2nd, 1951, was a wonderful day for me; the climax of a thrilling week and a great adventure. I can remember so well every minute of that day and every one of the preceding days. 3.15am was the important moment – I was lying, half-frozen with the cold, on the deck of the yacht Jasnar as she slipped across the finishing line of the 1950-51 Sydney-Hobart yacht race. For eight hours we (a crew of six) had been working our way up the Derwent River with just the faintest whisper of wind helping us on our way.

"We had sailed into Storm Bay the afternoon before after a glorious sail down the Tasmanian coast; we expected to cross the line within a few hours. A brisk sou'-easter had been blowing to beckon us on – on to Hobart and the finish of our 650-mile ocean race.

"The wind, however, left us and for a while we had not moved. Hobart lay ahead, tantalisingly near and seemingly so easy to reach. I lit a cigarette and the wisp of smoke went straight up into the clear air; the sails hung motionless. A whale swam lazily by – too close for comfort.

"Tensely we waited for the evening breeze. We changed Jasnar's ocean-going sails for her lighter gear and anxiously watched for telltale signs of the Derwent's famous light airs. The suspense was almost unbearable.

"Then as dusk fell a slight breeze touched our sails and sailing Jasnar like an open skiff, we entered the Derwent. Hobart disappeared in the dark and twinkling lights took its place. Gradually we worked our way up to the finishing line, excitement mounting as we slid through the water. Cold air came down from the summit of Mt Wellington and the stars above looked frosty and pale.

"For seven days we had battled with the elements; we had known the beauty and wonder of a small yacht fighting blustering winds, boisterous seas and now in the still calmness of a calm night we knew the pride and satisfaction of achievement. But we hadn't crossed the finishing line and tense with excitement we worked and waited, scarcely daring to breath.

"A light flashed continually from the line and suddenly we were across – the tension snapped and a wild exhilaration swept over me and with it, a deep feeling of peace. Unheeded tears rolled down my cheeks as I stood by myself in the bow realising that the race was over.

"That without a doubt was the most memorable day of my life. What followed when I went ashore is another story."

Ingate picks up on that story: "We got across the finishing line

Keith Wells demonstrates his sextant to a female admirer in Constitution Dock, watched by Sally and Gordon on the boom / INGATE FAMILY ARCHIVE

Sally the cook
INGATE FAMILY ARCHIVE

and were being towed into Constitution Dock and Boy Messenger is standing on the stern of Mistral II, having a pee. Sally is sitting beside me. Boy Messenger sings out at the top of his voice: 'Why don't you marry the girl?'

"At this stage Sally is engaged to John McLeod and I am sitting next to her steering the boat, being towed into Constitution Dock by this little motor boat. I looked around and said, 'What do you think of that, Sally?'

"She said, 'It's a very good idea, let's do it.'

"What are we going to do about John? She said, 'Don't worry I will look after that.'"

IN TELEGRAMS TO Colonel Saalfeld on January 3, Ingate wrote firstly:

"Passage up to expectations, not as hard as expected boat and crew performed excellently wear and tear only superficial. No sails torn or damaged. Broke light spinnaker pole. Carried away port lee runner, cross tree can be repaired. Seams showing on port side hard thrash on first days of race.

"Re engine have contacted agent only available from Sydney. Crew, self, suggest returning without engine save unnecessary expense please confirm.

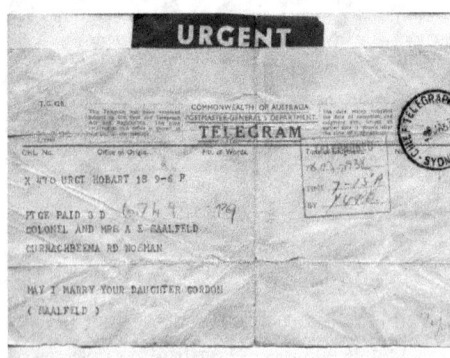

Gordon's telegram to Sally's parents
INGATE FAMILY ARCHIVE

"Will slip on Friday intend to start return trip on Monday cruise up coast 3 or 4 days then to Eden will confirm Saturday."

Then in a second telegram: "May I marry your daughter? – Gordon."

"The Colonel replied: 'Which one?' (The Saalfelds had two daughters; the younger one, Allene, was 16 years old).

"He knew that Sally was engaged to this other fella so he wasn't sure what it was all about," said Ingate.

ON THE RETURN voyage Jasnar, still without a motor, sailed through the Dunalley Canal for a shortcut exit from Storm Bay and had an uneventful passage until a 24-hour easterly gale hit off Wollongong. "The seas were amazing. We were on a lee shore and as we turned to sail through the Heads we faced white water. The seas were breaking right across the Heads and we came in like a bloody surfboat. I have never in all my sailing seen Sydney Heads as bad as that," said Ingate.

Although Sally, Gordon and the crew had held an engagement party at the then very new Wrest Point Hotel, when they returned to Sydney Colonel Saalfeld took Ingate aside and said, "Look, I'd like you to wait 12 months."

Sally later told him her father wanted to send her on a world trip. "I think the colonel was hoping she would get over me," said Ingate. "Halfway through the trip, she said, 'I can't stand this any longer,' came home and we got married."

Ingate sometime after the race queried Jasnar's rating with the Cruising Yacht Club of Australia's Commodore Merv Davey. Why had it been much higher for the smaller Jasnar than Jack Halliday's 34-footer Ellida? Davey re-calculated Jasnar's rating and found he had mis-recorded her foretriangle J measurement as 19ft when it was 16ft and she should have placed third on handicap corrected time instead of eighth after finishing tenth overall.

When Ingate asked if the placings were going to be altered, he said Davey replied, "The only way you can have anything changed is put in a protest and it's too late for protests."

In the winter of 1951, Jasnar had a tragic episode. On the return voyage to Sydney after a race to Newcastle in July, Bruce Jackson fell overboard about 2am on July 8, when Jasnar was off Catherine Hill Bay, in a strong westerly and smooth seas.

John Harvey, 27, of Mosman was on watch with Jackson. "Bruce was dozing in the cockpit," Ingate said. "Harvey, who was at the tiller, said that Bruce got up, stretched and fell. I was below as reserve watch when I heard a shout.

"Harvey threw a lifebelt in the direction of the voice and then we lit a flare. We were doing six knots under sail and it took us a while to turn back.

"We cruised for two hours searching for Bruce with our Aldis lamp

Gordon and Sally celebrate their engagement with Keith Wells at Wrest Point Hotel, Hobart / INGATE FAMILY ARCHIVE

and then we put back to Newcastle. Bruce was a fair swimmer but he was wearing a thick Air Force duffle coat and a hood over his other clothes because of the cold. I think the weight of his clothes stopped him swimming to us.

"I haven't spoken much about it all my life; nobody else saw him go. His father, a solicitor, was very upset and blamed me as skipper."

Ingate and Colonel Saalfeld continued sailing Jasnar. The colonel was a member of the Cruising Yacht Club of Australia in its earliest days and pivotal in its purchase of Cyril Kellshaw's boatshed in Rushcutters Bay in 1951, which became its first clubhouse. Half of the purchase price of £10,000 was raised by debentures for as little as 25 pounds from club members and the balance from a bank loan guaranteed by Colonel Saalfeld, Merv Davey and Vic Meyer.

Gordon Ingate joined the club in 1949 and in 2017 was its oldest member. His friend and former offshore crewmate Mick York joined in 1945. Ingate remembers: "Members had these old wooden lockers. We used to buy beer by the bottle and store it in our lockers so we could have a drink after our races."

Colonel Saalfeld sold Jasnar to John and Margaret Hearder who sailed it in Pittwater where they subsequently sold her to Jack Smyth, QC, who became Commodore of Royal Prince Alfred Yacht Club in 1956. "He sold the boat to Jack Parker, a furniture manufacturer, who had team of professionals fit out the interior and did a great job. The boat was then sold again to John Kinsella, a motor dealer who took up ocean racing with it again and was quite successful," said Ingate.

John's brother Phillip Kinsella took Jasnar over and in 1968 sailed her to Canada. In 1971, with Ian Millar joining Phillip Kinsella as owner, Jasnar again contested the Sydney-Hobart race.

Ingate was surprised to find on researching Jasnar's history, that she'd had at least 22 owners, including a nurse, Sarah Moore, who used her as a houseboat, moored off Gladesville Point, for a number of years.

Going aboard on June 3, 2016, for the first time since 1951, he was "also quite surprised to find she was in comparatively good condition, not a wreck. She has electric light, which we didn't have in 1950; a diesel engine and the batteries are in good condition. The compass is still mounted where we had it in 1950 on the bridge deck."

Gordon with Jasnar's damaged spreader, 67 years on / BOB ROSS

3

BUILDING THE HOUSE AND A BUSINESS

GORDON INGATE, WITH LITTLE FORMAL qualification, helped by his wife Sally, mother-in-law Nina and friends, from 1952 built a four-level house on a steep hillside property descending into Long Bay on Sydney's Middle Harbour. From that project, Ingate picked up skills that eventually led him into a profitable career in metal fabrication businesses, culminating with high-profile projects such as the Sydney Harbour tunnel and Centrepoint Tower, which financed his sailing ventures.

After gaining the Leaving Certificate at Sydney Boys High School, Paddington, 17-year-old Gordon went to work in the drawing division of the De Havilland Aircraft Company's engineering office.

Earlier, his father, who was very friendly with the general manager of the Water Board, had suggested Gordon go and see him about getting a job. The Water Board interviewed him and said it would like to send him to university to complete a degree in engineering. "I couldn't go to university, you had to have a foreign language, so I couldn't get that job."

After De Havilland, he joined the Commonwealth Experimental Building Station at North Ryde as a junior builder's labourer. Then he went to Sonnerdal Pty Ltd, a Swedish-owned company that made the gears for the Holden cars in the 1950s as a time and motion engineer then moved to Tutt Bryant, an earth-moving company, for a higher salary offer.

When that job ended in the 1952 Depression, Ingate began working for car dealer Norman G. Booth, a champion Dragon class sailor, as a used car salesman. His boss was Carl Ryves; Dick Sargeant was there as a motor mechanic and Peter ('Poddy') O'Donnell, married to a daughter of Booth, was also on the payroll.

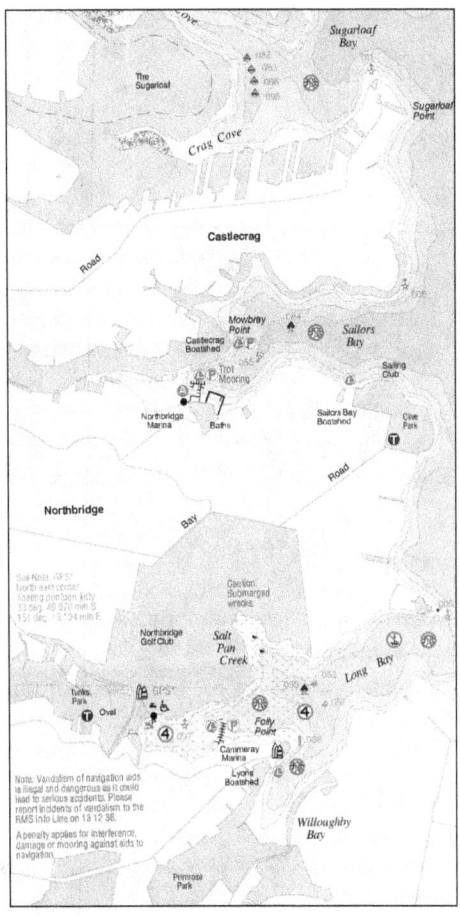

Upper Middle Harbour including Long Bay
NSW ROADS AND MARITIME SERVICES

All three had represented Australia at the Olympic Games. "The whole idea was if Norm wanted to train during the week he'd just say to the boys, 'OK, we are going sailing.' After six months I told Norm, 'I can't do this.'"

Gordon and Sally, who had been married for two years, were living at his mother's house in Willoughby, planned to build their own house on the Cammeray waterfront hillside. "I said to Sally, 'I have given up the job.' She said, 'What are you going to do?' And I said, 'I think I will start building the house.'

"I didn't know what I was letting myself in for. My mother found this

Nina Saalfeld and Sally were the main helpers
INGATE FAMILY ARCHIVE

block of land and on Sundays I used to organise some of the sailing crew to come down and do a bit of work cleaning up the property; chopping trees down. I would put on a barbecue, fill up a small keg with beer and we'd have beer and sausages."

Gordon's uncle Cliff Hodgson, a builder, looked at the site and told him he should sell it. "It's too steep, the mudflats at low tide are going to smell. Take a loss on it if necessary, but sell."

"While a close friend, Adrian Cox, became supervising architect, a young fellow serving his time for my grandfather, T.W.Hodgson did the drawings for free."

"We engaged an engineer, recommended by the architect's office who said, 'You have to put down six columns that go down to rock. You'll know when you are into rock when you put a crow bar down and it goes 'ding'. So, I reached a stage where I was 18ft down a 3ft square hole – a long way – filling a bucket with soil and Sally would haul it up and tip it down the slope to where the swimming pool is now at the bottom of the property and I did six holes.

"I was paying my mother rent to live in

Work and fun, clearing the hillside

her house at Willoughby on not much income. With the money I had saved from Norman G. Booth, Tutt Bryant and other jobs I had bought a builder's truck, paid for the block and I was broke.

"Mrs Saalfeld introduced me to her bank manager, from the Commercial Bank of Sydney, in Mosman. I found out that he used to drink at the Buena Vista hotel on Saturday. I met him there after sailing, told him what I was doing and he said he would come along and have a look. He saw a cleared block and the six holes I was about to fill up with concrete and said he would give 1000 pounds for the concrete. I think the concrete for the six holes was 750 pounds. The house was built on overdraft, not the usual mortgage, using 46,000 bricks.

"I got a bricklayer to come down and give me a price at so much a thousand. When the bricklayer turned up on the very first day, he said, 'Okay mate, where do we start?'

"A professional builder was building a house next door and I went and

Sally loading bricks on the chute down to the site
INGATE FAMILY ARCHIVE

Neighbourhood children helped
INGATE FAMILY ARCHIVE

Bricklaying at ground level
INGATE FAMILY ARCHIVE

asked his foreman, and he said, 'Start at the doorway downstairs'. So I became the builder. Whenever I was stuck, I would go and ask him. So, with the help of Sally and her mother – the two best ladies you could ever have – and my friends on Sundays, we built the house. It took us a long time, around seven years and it's still not finished."

Gordon intended putting Malthoid tarred paper on the roof, which was standard in those days, but his bank manager insisted that it could not be used. Tiles would not work on a flat roof, concrete was too heavy, copper was too costly.

"A copper roof would cost all the money I had spent to that stage. Because I had worked at De Havilland Aircraft, I knew a little bit about aluminium and got to know

The structure takes shape
INGATE FAMILY ARCHIVE

some of the guys at Australuco, the Australian aluminium company and asked them what were the chances of using aluminium instead of copper on a roof. They said if I used aluminium that was 99 per cent pure it should last as long as copper providing, I didn't associate any dissimilar metals with it. We worked out a price on rolled aluminium and it was fantastic, a lot cheaper than copper."

"Geoff Peacock, who used to sail at the CYCA, had a business called Alucraft which made aluminium tiles looked at the idea and said it would work; we would have to find someone to do it. We were starting from scratch and I said, 'Why can't I do it?'"

Ingate and his helpers laid the roof with aluminium sheets about 3ft wide, folded up at the edges over wooden battens and with aluminium capping pieces over the joins.

Completion with a fabulous view
INGATE FAMILY ARCHIVE

"So, with a couple of crewmates, we hammered the roof on. And it's still there as brand new, without deterioration in any way. The people living opposite, above us, complained because the reflection was disturbing them so I had to paint it after it was three or four years on. To the best of my knowledge it was the first flat aluminium roof in Sydney and I used aluminium for the gutters and downpipes."

That roof set Ingate off on his profitable path in lightweight structural engineering. "We were working on the roof one Sunday when a guy walked along the single dirt track and asked us what we were doing? 'Putting an aluminium roof on this house.'

"He said, 'I am an architect and have a building that could do with this sort of roof, I have already made enquiries about an aluminium roof being formed in Switzerland, would you be interested in giving me a price?'"

The building was the Coogee telephone exchange. "My mate

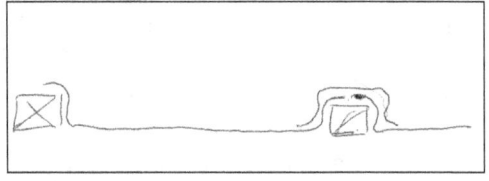

How the aluminium roofing sheets were joined

The finished roof, 67 years on

John Nippard and I drove over to Coogee and got the shock of our lives when we saw the size of the building; it was a bloody big building. He accepted the price and that started us in business and I stayed in the aluminium fabrication business until 1967."

With the help of the banker, Ingate started to get work in aluminium roofing. He didn't have the money start his own business so joined Bob Knowland in forming Lightweight Structures in 1954.

"That's where I made my first boo boo. I joined up with a bloke who put in 75 per cent while I put in 25 per cent. You never go into business with someone unless you've got 55 per cent."

On October 1, 1960, Ingate told Bob Knowland that if he wouldn't allow him to increase his shareholding in Lightweight Structures, would he mind if he invested in Rigby Jones, a metal fabrication company started by Sam Rigby and John Jones.

Knowland agreed and Ingate, while remaining as general manager of Lightweight Structures, became an investor in Rigby Jones with a 51 per cent shareholding while Rigby and Jones held 49 percent between them. "I was still working for Lightweight Structures building aluminium roofs and aluminium boats, by the way. Everything I convinced Bob Knowland to do made him money until 1967 when he started complaining he was paying too much tax."

"It upset me to think Mr Knowland sacked me because of my spending too much time sailing when 90 per cent of Lightweight Structures' work came from my connections at the Royal Sydney Yacht Squadron."

RIGBY JONES STARTED in a small factory with 12 men and Sam Rigby and John Jones as sub-contractors. "Sam Rigby was a first grade Rugby Union player with the Eastern Suburbs club and we got a lot of work from his Rugby Union connections.

"The business grew and within two years we were looking at buying a block of land out at Smithfield and building a bigger factory. We moved out to Smithfield in 1962. At this stage we were employing

30 people and getting more and more work."

An early contract was to install aluminium roofing on the overseas passenger terminal at Circular Quay in Sydney. "I knew this English firm had produced roll-formed roofing sheets and roll forming was better than being pressed. They gave me a good price. Lightweight Structures installed the aluminium roofing imported from England.

One of the best contracts was to line the interior of Sydney's Centrepoint Tower with corrugated iron and constructing the steel stairwell.

A special problem was stress relieving the welds. "They welded it, then I attached huge electrical wires to the electrical system of Sydney and when they turned the power on, it brought this enormous steel ring up to red heat and then they allowed it to cool."

The Ingate house (centre) on the crowded Cammeray Hillside / BOB ROSS

Ingate was also still working for Lightweight Structures when it gained the contract for lining the Cahill Expressway tunnel with an aluminium ceiling. Alan George, who was Ingate's main foreman at Lightweight Structures, came up with the idea of using corrugated aluminium sheeting that would remain airproof and could go around a curve, hung from the tunnel's series of overhead concrete beams. Johnny Jones and Sam Rigby devised a method of fixing the sheeting to the beams.

"We put a price in for the job and signed a contract. We finished the job and made a very handsome profit out of it for Bob Knowland's Lightweight Structures. I got a bonus big enough to buy Caprice of Huon with Mrs Saalfeld. The worst part was, the price was about 110,000 pounds and the chief engineer for the job said, 'You've done a great job, Gordon. If your price had been doubled, you still would have got the contract.'

"This upset the boss, Bob Knowland. Rigby Jones had made it all out of aluminium. Lightweight Structures didn't have an engineering shop like Rigby Jones had. He was upset because I had not only made a lot of money for Lightweight Structures; I had made a lot for Rigby Jones.

"Then I got the contract for Lightweight Structures to make a huge, 56-acre wool store roof out at Padstow. "I got the job for Lightweight Structures but was fired before we actually did it."

Bob Knowland sacked Ingate in 1967 after Ingate took up an offer from Sir Frank Packer to skipper Gretel in the America's Cup selection trials.

"When I got fired from Lightweight Structures I said to Sam Rigby and Johnny Jones, "Your business is going quite well and I think it should employ me. My job will be to increase the business; I will not be a drag on the company and we are going to be able to pay my salary.

"And that's exactly how it started. All my contacts at the Royal Sydney Yacht Squadron led to tremendous business. Rigby Jones just built up and the factory at Smithfield grew bigger and bigger"

Ingate excelled at networking, and a conversation with one of his cousins, Cliff Hodgson, who worked for Wunderlich, a German company that made pressed metal patterned ceilings, led to him recruiting Wunderlich's works manager Jack Stone.

"He was works manager at Wunderlich with 4,000 workers, and came to Rigby Jones when I think we had 50 employees. When I sold the business in 1999 it had 132 employees. Rigby Jones grew because of the demand on their ability to cut, bend, roll metal materials up to one inch thick."

THE BREAKTHROUGH WITH aluminium roofing afforded Ingate's purchase of the Dragon Class Sea Fever, with Mrs Saalfeld, in 1955.

Ingate's association with Rigby Jones ended in 1999 when he was involved in negotiating a contract with a French company's Tomago aluminium centre at Raymond Terrace and became involved in a dispute with the boilermakers' association.

"The boilermakers put the pressure on by saying, 'We need a million dollars from Rigby Jones into our bank account so that if you go broke there will be money to pay the men.'

"The boilermakers' president said, 'If you don't agree to our proposal, we'll shut you down on Monday.' This was Friday afternoon, about four o'clock and I said, 'You are not going to shut us down, I will shut up shop'. And then I sacked all the people. I think we employed 100 men."

Ingate then sold Rigby Jones to Peter Smaller who was running a similar business in South Africa. "He came over to Australia because of South Africa's political problems, saw the for-sale notice, paid us the money we wanted; very fortunate."

Rigby Jones joined the Southern Steel Group in 2000.

During the years building up Lightweight Structures, completion of the Ingates' house slowed. The garage on the roof level did not go on until four or five years after the Ingates began living there.

Another rainbow had popped out of Gordon's arse not long after he bought the land on which to build the house in 1952. Opposite, across Long Bay, was a golf course and bush-clad hillside parkland, never to be built on, but the waters on this head of the bay were heavily polluted.

"When I bought this place 66 years ago, Cowdroy Avenue was a single dirt track with very few other houses in the street. It was overlooking mud flats with mangrove swamps all the way to the Tunks Park bridge at the head of the bay.

"Raw sewage from Willoughby and Chatswood was coming into the bay. I did not know that until low tide. I bought this land at high tide with the nor'easter blowing but when the wind dropped the smell was unbearable.

"I was told I should take a loss and sell immediately, which I didn't. Not long after, the council installed a sewerage pipe, about 12 inches in diameter and the smell disappeared."

Then, one day, a dredge turned up in the bay and anchored opposite Ingate's block. It had sailed out from Holland to deepen Newcastle Harbour to accommodate big ships. The captain told Ingate they wanted to dredge out the headwaters of Long Bay to make sure the dredging equipment was still working. So, he anchored opposite the Ingates' block, put down a six-inch diameter pipe, dredged out the mangroves and the mud to create Tunks Park.

Another rainbow.

4

DRAGONS, FIRST FORAY

WHILE GORDON INGATE MADE HISTORY as the oldest skipper to win the Prince Philip Cup Australian Dragon class championship, at the age of 90 in 2017, after previous wins in 2015 and 2009, his successful career in Dragons began much earlier.

In 1948, when he was in his twenties and winning NSW championships in the Vee Ess dinghy class, he began receiving invitations to steer Dragons, including George Bate's Marjorie Anne, a freakishly fast boat. Bate was a bricklayer and carpenters from his building team built her honestly but, Ingate believes, longer on the waterline than she should have been.

The Norwegian designer and boatbuilder, Johan Anker, designed the 29ft Dragon in 1923 as a family racer for a crew of three. The class quickly took hold on the neighbouring shores of Germany, Norway and Holland and in 1935 reached the Clyde in Scotland and in 1938, England. In 1948, as the class continued to spread in numbers throughout the world, it was chosen as three-man keelboat for the Olympic sailing at Torquay.

The Australian International Dragon Association records that Jack Linacre of Melbourne was the first person in Australia to start building a Dragon, from plans he found in a Uffa Fox book, with a small cabin for cruising around Port Phillip Bay, as well as racing. He laid the keel in his mother's backyard. The first Australian Dragon launched was Sea Joy, built by Alan Jarman in Sydney in 1950, which unfortunately didn't measure. Jarman persisted with other Sea Joys and in 1960 won the Prince Philip Cup with Sea Joy IV.

Ingate and his wife Sally, supported by his mother-in-law Nina Saalfeld, decided to have a Dragon built. In 1953 they were part of a group of Sydney yachtsmen, with Ingate unofficial leader, intent on building Dragons, which decided to get bulk quotes on materials and sails to keep costs down.

A more-or-less uniform set of specs was hammered out and each prospective owner sought builder's quotes ranging from £1,200 to £1,600. The group got together again to work out where money could be saved by ordering keels, sails and fittings in quantity. Mass production would halve the cost of the ballast keel. The pattern would cost them £54 which, divided among ten, amounted to a little more than a fiver a keel.

Eventually six new boats were on the stocks; the first almost ready for launching mid-1953. The Ingates' Sea Fever II, launched in 1955, was the 23rd Dragon to be launched in New South Wales. She cost about £2,000.

Sid Ferguson and Billy Barnett built her in Oregon planking fastened by galvanised steel nails, in a waterfront shed at Lavender Bay on Sydney Harbour. "They used to fight while they were building the boat," Ingate recalls. "Why don't you do it this way?" Billy Barnett would say.

"Don't be silly, you silly old redhead," Ferguson would reply.

Barnett went on to build 10 Dragons after establishing his own boatshed in Berry's Bay.

"It was quite different to the other Dragons," said Ingate. "I decided to go for a light keel – the cast iron keel was the lightest possible in the rules – and a very small, tiny, cockpit, the smallest you could have by the rules. I have no idea why because today you go for practically maximum cockpit, maximum weight and now they are built in fibreglass although there are some wooden boats that would still beat the newest fibreglass boats."

Ingate learned valuable lessons from top Dragon sailors of the time.

Sea Fever II / INGATE FAMILY ARCHIVE

"The first race in Dragons I came last; the second race in the Dragons I came second last.

"Archie Robertson came up to me and said, 'Gordon, you should be doing a lot better than you are; what you are trying to do is win.'

"I said, 'yeah, isn't that the idea?'

"'No, try and come second; pick the guy who is winning and follow him.'

"So next race, the guy I followed was Archie; he came first and I came second. Never forget that whoever is doing well, go where they're going. From that day I thought I am sailing the boat alright, I was just going the wrong way."

Another Dragon sailor of the time to influence Ingate, and indeed the whole Sydney fleet, was Eric Strain, from Northern Ireland, who had finished fourth in the Dragon class at the 1948 Olympics representing Great Britain. Strain came to Sydney in 1952 to sell advertising for Seacraft magazine. Colin Ryrie, who had just won the Australian 12ft skiff championship with Norman Longworth as his lightweight well hand, met him at the ship and soon took him crewing on his 12ft skiff in a black nor'easter.

"We gave him a rather hard time," said Longworth, "But he quickly showed he was capable. From that time forward, Eric seemed determined to persuade Colin and myself to go into one-design keelboats, particularly Dragons, as opposed to development boats."

Before Longworth and later Ryrie got into Dragons, they sailed Finns, the Olympic singlehander, introduced to Sydney Harbour in 1954 and vied for selection in the Australian team for the 1956 Olympics in Melbourne. Ryrie won selection and stayed in Finns until he took up Dragon sailing in a serious way in 1965. Longworth had moved to Dragons long before that, saying, "I decided there was a much easier way to go sailing."

Longworth sailed some races with Strain on Australian Dragon class pioneer Alan Jarman's Sea Joy II and then, aged 26, bought Marjorie

Sydney fleet start, 1956 / INGATE FAMILY ARCHIVE

Sea Fever II heads right on Botany Bay / INGATE FAMILY ARCHIVE

Anne, DKA6. "I had a bit of trouble getting performance early so Eric Strain sailed the boat for me. We won the Prince Philip Cup in Sydney in 1959 – I sailed in the middle and up forward – using Peter Cole and Joe Pearce sails. This was significant because this was the first year of synthetic sail cloth in Dragons and everyone else had been using (imported from England) Ratsey & Lapthorne cotton sails."

Longworth and Strain took Marjorie Anne to Melbourne in 1960 for the Prince Philip Cup and the Olympic trials. They won the Prince Philip Cup from Alan Jarman's Sea Joy IV.

Strain, because he had represented Great Britain at the 1948 Olympics was ineligible for the Olympic trials that followed. Longworth skippered Marjorie Anne to finish third in the trials behind Melbourne boat Ghost, skippered by Mick Brooke and Sea Joy IV.

Believing that Marjorie Anne had lost a bit of shape, Longworth, in 1960 had Bill Barnett build Basilisk. "It was the first mahogany boat that Billy built," said Longworth. "Eric Strain had a lot of input and like Marjorie Anne, she proved to be a light weather flier.

"However, Marjorie Anne went on to get a second in the Prince Philip Cup on Cockburn Sound (WA) a couple of years later, which horrified Eric and which only went to prove that there's no such thing as light-weather boat or a heavy-weather boat in Dragons; only light weather sail trimmers and skippers and heavy weather skipper/trimmers."

Strain had a pronounced influence not only on the Dragon class, but also on Australian attitudes to one-design keelboat racing generally. He was scornful of ocean racing, which dominated the newspaper coverage of sailing at the time, describing it as "unscientific bullocking". And he said of the Saturday Sydney Harbour mixed handicap racing fleets: "They should go for a little sail in the morning and then anchor in orderly fashion off Bradleys, at a respectable distance, watch the real yacht racing (meaning in Dragons) and learn something."

Longworth says: "He was a character; full of dry humour. His idea of two fingers of whisky were fingers vertical, not horizontal. But he was a marvellous helmsman. Probably his greatest feat was in the mid-1960s when we had 22 Dragons racing every Saturday. In one season Eric sailed something like 17 different boats and had 14 wins.

"He was runner-up in both the 1968 and 1972 Olympic trials with Mike Fletcher in the well and I think the technical input of Fletcher and the steering capability of Eric resulted in Mike Fletcher going to the '72 Games as boatman, but unofficially as coach and subsequently Mike Fletcher was the Olympic coach."

Strain won four NSW titles and with Mike Ramsden in the middle and Fletcher on the bow finished second in the 1972 Olympic trials, a point behind the Queenslanders John Cuneo, Tom Anderson and John Shaw, who went on to win the gold medal at Kiel. Fletcher, selected as reserve, especially helped Cuneo with his Dragon at Kiel, re-cutting his sails and advising him how to re-set the rig.

Longworth continued: "Eric must be credited with turning yachting around in Australia to make it a highly-competitive one-design nation. At the time and still in some parts of Australian yachting today it's a case of 'I can buy a faster boat than yours,' cheque book yachting. There's no doubt the one-design principle, properly regulated, put an end to that nonsense."

Gordon Ingate was also greatly influenced by the way Eric Strain sailed a Dragon. "With the Dragons you can get alongside another boat and go for hours at the same speed. But one bad tack and you can lose three boats because they are inherently slow," he says. The long keel has a leading edge that looks like a brick and what happens is the Dragon allows for tactical sailing because it's slow.

"Because the Dragons are so slow, the headsails are full; literally designed like the old-fashioned ballooner they used to have on the 16s and the 18s. So you are not going high like you do in the Etchells, you are going fast, as fast as you can do in a Dragon, which is about five and a-quarter knots.

"Anyone who has spent a fair amount of time on the water sailing a Dragon just develops techniques. Eric Strain had the feel for a Dragon; he could point a Dragon so high compared to anybody else. He knew exactly

Sea Fever II in a pin-end start on Sydney Harbour / INGATE FAMILY ARCHIVE

when he was too high; he knew exactly when his speed was dropping. He became practically unbeatable because he had the feel for a Dragon.

"He had a tremendous touch on the helm of a Dragon. He could pinch and pinch much better than anyone else and still keep the boat moving. I think I learned a lot from that because that's the way I sail today."

BACK IN 1956, Ingate's first big event was a selection series on Botany Bay to choose two boats to represent New South Wales in the trials to select the Australian Olympic team trials in Melbourne. The boatbuilders and experienced sailors Sid Ferguson and Billy Barnett crewed for him. "It blew like the clappers for the whole seven-race series and all I can say is between the three of us, we kept the boat afloat," Ingate said.

Sea Fever II finished third behind Pel (Bill Fesq) and Sea Joy III (Alan Jarman) but beat seasoned campaigners Norman G. Booth and Archie Robertson despite the windy conditions not suiting her.

That encouraged Ingate to enter the Prince Philip Cup to be held in Melbourne straight after the Olympics, knowing the Olympic fleet would be set up for stronger winds. "I thought I might be lucky enough to get a light weather series, which in fact we did."

Just getting the boat to Melbourne was a challenge for Ingate. He borrowed George Bate's 30cwt truck and trailer and towed Sea Fever II there on his own, down the Hume Highway that was then largely unsealed.

"The trailer had no mudguards and the boat was a bloody mess when we got there," said Ingate. "Every seam was cracked and her rudder was damaged. We jammed putty into her in a hurry, slapped paint on and launched her when it was still wet."

In the last-minute rush to rig the boat, Ingate and crew stepped the mast plumb instead of raking it four inches astern from the perpendicular in its previous setting. That helped the boat's light weather performance.

Joining Ingate were two experienced Sydney crewmen, Paul Edds, who skippered his own Dragon, as forward hand and Walter Haines from Marjorie Anne as main hand.

Sea Fever II had been launched with a suit of Ratsey & Lapthorn sails. Inspired by his success with Peter Cole sails in the Vee Esses, Ingate had Cole build him a suit for the Dragon to race with in Melbourne. "I asked him to make a suit of sails that would go well in light weather and said they had to be full.

"And that is why we did so well because it was a seven-race light weather series. The water on Port Phillip was flat and we had beautiful breeze coming in either from the south-east or west. It was great and we were literally able to go faster than any boat other than Pel."

The fleet of 20 included five Dragons that had sailed in the Olympics, including bronze medallist Bluebottle, the Duke of Edinburgh', Dragon

Sea Fever II covered in mud after the tow to Melbourne
INGATE FAMILY ARCHIVE

Pel leads Sea Fever II in the Prince Philip Cup sail-off on Sydney Harbour / INGATE FAMILY ARCHIVE

skippered by Graham Mann, which finished fifth.

The last race was sailed in a light southerly, with Sea Fever II among five boats positioned to win the series. Fourth at the first mark, Sea Fever II improved on each leg to win comfortably and with Pel fourth and worst placings discarded, finish the series in an unbreakable tie with Pel. Sea Fever II had 3-4-4-8-1 placings for 4091 points to Pel's 4-3-6-1-4 (4091).

After winning the last race, Ingate hung around the committee boat, watching the other finishers. "I told my crew, 'I think we have a chance of winning this.' Bill Fesq had already pulled off the course and gone back to Brighton. I asked the finishing team, 'How did we do?' And they said, 'We are trying to work it out, but it looks like you've tied with Bill Fesq.'

"By the time we got back to Brighton to tell Bill – it was a fair way in – his mast was out and he was packing up to go back to Sydney. We said, 'Bill, we have to sail off.' He said, 'No, I don't want that; you have the Cup.'"

The deed of gift of the Prince Philip Cup prevented that and eventually, Fesq and Ingate agreed to have a one-race sail-off on January 31, 1957, on Sydney Harbour.

The sail-off was an anti-climax. Firstly, with a 20-knot nor'-easter forecast, Ingate chose to race with his tired Ratsey & Lapthorn sails when, with the breeze moderating, Cole sails would have been more effective.

And then, his starting tactics were wrong. "I went out in January 1957 not very confidently because I had never heard of match racing and what I know today I didn't know then. I knew exactly what I was going to do; duck his stern on port tack at the start, sail on four or five boat lengths and then tack back on starboard in a controlling position."

Pel's massive winning margin in the Prince Philip sail-off / INGATE FAMILY ARCHIVE

But, as every Sydney Harbour club racer knows in a nor'-easter, from starting lines north east of Clarke Island, the conventional wisdom is to start on starboard and sail straight to Bradley's Head to pick up the port-tack wind shift always found off this large promontory.

"That is exactly what Bill Fesq did. He didn't tack until he got to the rocks at Bradley's Head, tacked on the permanent shift there and was in front. He just sat on me from there and won by nearly two minutes."

AFTER TWO SEASONS in Dragons, Ingate seized an opportunity to move into the International 5.5 metre class, went on to represent Australia in the 1965 Admiral's Cup international offshore teams racing championship, won selection for Australia in the Tempest class at the 1972 Olympics; campaigned Gretel II for the 1977 America's Cup and continued to sail her until 1989, before returning to the Dragon class in 1994.

5

5.5 METRES

INGATE SOLD HIS DRAGON SEA Fever II for a good price in 1959 and with Mrs Saalfeld bought the 5.5 metre Kirribilli, the Jan Linge design Royal Sydney Yacht Squadron members funded which Pat Taylor sailed in the 1956 Olympic trials. She was narrowly beaten by Buraddoo (Jock Sturrock), which went on to win the bronze medal at the Melbourne Games.

The 5.5 metre is a three-man restricted keelboat class developed soon after World War Two mainly by Charles Nicholson (designer of the Endeavour J boats) and Major Heckstall-Smith. Length is unrestricted but usually between 30ft to 35ft within the measurement rule which has encouraged a relatively shallow, light, canoe body with a separate fin. "They're a bit like a Twelve Metre," says Ingate, "You can have a small fat one or a long, skinny one." The rudder had to be attached to the after end of the keel until the rule was changed from January 1, 1970. The 5.5 was sailed in the Olympics from 1952 to 1968, after which it retained a strong international following, particularly in the Scandinavian countries.

"They are beautiful to steer, very light and easy on the helm," says Ingate. "Like any sailing boat, that depends on how you set the mast and the sails. I used to hear people say, 'I've got weather helm,' but it's only because the mast isn't correctly raked. The spinnakers are the right size for the boat. The 5.5s don't get into much trouble when the wind is fresh, freshening or frightening.

"From the moment I picked up Kirribilli, I enjoyed the class; its people as well as the boat. And we built it up from basically nothing. I became Australian 5.5 Association class secretary mainly because I was enthusiastic about developing the class, which was already popular overseas. In 1964-65, after Bill Northam won Olympic gold and the world championship in Tokyo, the fives became very popular in Australia. At one stage we had 40 boats.

"When the Squadron decided to go into the 5.5s in 1954, they insisted, 'We must not have any mistakes. Make sure that the boat measures.' And I think that was the best decision ever made because from there on, any boat being measured; whether it was Dragons, 5.5s, J24s, the Squadron boats always measured correctly when that didn't apply to other boats. Some people did try to fiddle with the rules but that was nipped in the bud pretty quickly."

Altair arriving in Australia from England / INGATE FAMILY ARCHIVE

INGATE, WITH MIKE Ramsden and Mick Morris crewing, and no other opposition in Sydney, sent Kirribilli to Melbourne for a series to select the Australian representative for the 1960 Olympic sailing regatta on the Bay of Naples. Close friend Austin Edwards, owner of the show-

Kirribili launch, Royal Sydney Yacht Squadron, 1956 / INGATE FAMILY ARCHIVE

piece yacht Margaret Rintoul, generously provided the transport and Mrs Saalfeld bought them a new Herbulot spinnaker. "There were just the two boats," said Ingate, "The fleet that had been there for the trials in 1956 had dissipated and the 5.5s had yet to catch on in Sydney."

Buraddoo, better suited to the strong winds on Port Phillip, won 12 consecutive races in the trials. "When it blows hard on Port Phillip, it blows very hard and Jock had the better boat for heavy weather," said Ingate. "I suggested we swap boats for the last race next day. We did and it was light weather and he beat me again. I said to Jock after that race, 'the weather forecast for Naples is light weather. I don't want any money for it but I think you should take my boat because it's a super light weather boat.'

"He said, 'Thanks Gordon but I know how to sail Buraddoo'. I am sure I can do better with Burradoo'. He goes over to Naples and finishes 10th out of 19 boats (placings 4-12-2-13-14-12-18). The boat that won was a sister ship to Kirribilli, designed by Jan Linge, designer of the Soling and Yngling."

Ingate with Kirribilli won the 1960-61 and 1961-62 Australian 5.5 metre championships on Pittwater. He sold her in 1962 to South Australian Rex Godfrey but continued racing in the class, steering his friend Hugh Hamilton's Kaiami. Designed by Arvid Lauren of Sweden, Kiaimi was built by Woodnutts on the Isle of Wight in 1955 and named

Altair. Bill Furber, of Royal Prince Edward YC, Sydney, bought her to sail in the Cowes regatta and the Australian selection trials for the 1956 Olympics in which she finished third. She was the first 5.5m registered in Australia. She then became owned by Tony Carr of Royal Prince Alfred Yacht Club, about 1960, and carried the sail number AUS 001. Carr had a second 5.5 built, designed by Elnar Ohlson and built by Billy Barnett in Sydney, in 1962, which was also named Altair and carried the KA1 sail number. When Carr sold the original Altair to Hugh Hamilton, he insisted that he keep the name for his new boat, so Hamilton re-named the original Altair Kaiami, an extension of the original sail number (KA1). She became registered as KA15.

Hauled to travel, Mosman Bay, 1960
INGATE FAMILY ARCHIVE

INGATE TOOK KAIAMI out of the water for four months, completely refitted and re-rigged her to save about 200lb in weight, invested in a new mainsail by Peter Cole and a new jib and spinnaker by Bob Miller (later renamed Ben Lexcen).

Going into the 1964 Olympic selection trials on Lake Macquarie, with around 30 starters, Ingate rated Kaiami as fourth favourite, behind Jock Sturrock in the new Ohlson design Pam owned by Royal St Kilda Yacht Club Commodore Otto Meik, Norman G. Booth in the Ray Hunt design Southern Cross, and Bill Northam's new Bill Luders design Barranjoey.

Barranjoey, with Northam, crewed by experienced campaigners Dick Sargeant and Pod O'Donnell, fresh from sailing on the 1962 America's Cup challenger Gretel, won the trials sensationally. Going into the last race of the seven-race series Barranjoey had to finish first or second to

win Olympic team selection. Third on the beat to the finish, she broke away from the two leaders, Pam and Southern Cross, sailed into stronger breeze and a favourable shift on the Lake's north-east shore, to climb to second behind Pam and win the series. When Northam dropped his worst placing, a seventh, his six-race points total was 5126. When Sturrock dropped his worst placing, a fourth, his total was 4950. Booth was a close third with 4598 and Ingate fourth. "There was a big gap between Kiaimi, fifth, sixth and seventh but we fought and had some bloody good races on Lake Macquarie," said Ingate.

THERE WAS STILL resistance to Northam's selection, led by the Victorians who reminded the Australian Yachting Federation that it did not necessarily have to have to send the winner of the trials to the Olympics, that Northam, aged 59, was too old, not medal material and the experienced campaigner Sturrock should go to Tokyo. "It was terrible, being the association secretary," said Ingate. "We had to work hard to get Northam there and Jock and I fell out because of that. So Northam goes off and wins, even though he was carrying a did-not-finish placing after a rules altercation."

Above and opposite: Kirribilli on the wind
INGATE FAMILY ARCHIVE

Northam sailed an excellent series helped by his great crew and his own shrewd brand of gamesmanship. In recounting his win, he used to suggest that he needled Sargeant and O'Donnell to excellence. But Dick Sargeant said: "I don't want to spoil a good story, but Bill was very good with us, the quietest skipper ever. We got on really well together. He'd let us do whatever we wanted with sail selection and trim. Pod would call most of the tactics and Bill would just steer the boat, but he steered well.

"He would concentrate more than anyone I have ever sailed with going to windward. He gave it the lot, pointing with the best of them and footing with the best of them, so intent on his steering all the time that when he got to the weather mark, you'd have to tell him whether to turn left or right."

Bill Northam's own account of the Tokyo Games, published in the 1973 Rigby book The Sailing Australians as told to Bob Ross, recalled

Kirribilli under spinnaker
INGATE FAMILY ARCHIVE

that his selection "was a lively issue at the time and I left with a doubtful honour for Tokyo. The newspapers were hard, too. I remember the night we left, John Crosbie, the manager and I left early to line things up over there. We were hanging about at Mascot, feeling a little foolish in our Panama hats and uniforms and only my five grandchildren came to see me off. An hour after we were flying, Crosbie showed me a newspaper. He hadn't been game to give it to me before. It said, 'Why did they send a no-hoper like Northam, the bloke's too old, he'll never see it through.'

"And that attitude was taken up by a lot of people. I played on it when we got to Enoshima, where the Olympic yachting was held. Different ones would come up to me and say, 'Are you the manager?' and I'd say, 'No I'm the rubber-downer' so they didn't know where they were. Tell them nothing and get as many goats as you can because the more blokes you fight with, the more they'll be looking out for you on the water, trying to get you instead of sailing their boats.

"I had to fight for permission to get our crew to Japan early. I had collected all the weather reports for 30 years but everyone told me that Enoshima waters were very tricky. We arrived there ten days earlier than the other nations and I consider that made all the difference. We were the first boat on the water, out even before the Japanese. So we were well broken in. Then a cyclone hit the place, which kept the late-comers ashore for a week.

"We'd trained hard before we left Australia, too. I was always frightened I'd go in the legs, as you do when you get old. I had to make sure they'd stand up to the jumping around in the slippery hull of Barranjoey. So for four months before we left, I was up at half past five, running and walking, every morning. The local shopkeepers used to cop it from their wives. 'Why don't you get out like that old bloke and run some of that weight off?' they'd say. The shopkeepers have put my prices up ever since. But we were all fit and if you are physically fit, you are mentally fit. The Olympics are a big strain. You've got to be able to give it, and you've got to be able to take it.

"For the three or four weeks we were there, we did an awful lot of sailing; seven hours a day, and even when the cyclone was approaching and the seas got really rough, the boys still made me do six hours a day. And it was very, very hot. I lost a stone and a-half during the time I was in Japan. Just before the races I went down with what I thought was pneumonia and it could have been a bad dose of the 'flu. For three days I was a really sick bloke. They sent me down drugs that I couldn't take because of my ulcer.

"We won the first race and only lost the points lead once, after about the third race. Then we got it back again with a win. Our record was three firsts, a second, third, fourth and a disqualification. The disqualification in the fifth race put us in an awkward position and it was my lapse. We'd been covering Straulino, the Italian, for 30 minutes and rounding the mark I forgot all about him as we went for the spinnaker. And bang, he was up on me.

"By then it was down to Don McNamara, the American and us. He had a good reputation as a skipper and two good fellows with him although they were not as good as mine. His Luders boat was almost identical to mine, the only difference being two portholes in the side of his. He wanted me to have a look at the boat before the races. When I

Bill Northam with Barranjoey, Lake Macquarie, 1964 / GORDON INGATE

asked about the portholes, he said, 'You'll see. You are not going to know what I am doing but I'll be able to see what you are doing through these.'

"'Well, I said, 'You've got 'em in the wrong place, Mac. 'You'd better put them in the bow if you want to follow what we're doing; they're no good on the side.'

"He never forgave me for that one. And going out to the starts, we'd get alongside and sing 'McNamara's Band' and he'd get really mad. He's a really serious bloke. The two boys didn't go along with this and I said, 'It's alright boys, you just leave the brainwork to me and just do the rope jerking and I'll show you how this can be worked.' And there's no doubt about it, McNamara spent most of his time watching me instead of what he was doing.

"I felt the pressure too, towards the end. When we started, I thought we could win a medal but had no idea it would be a gold. Every race, when it became apparent we were going so well, the others were making it more difficult for me. I was getting to feel tired and develop aches. I'd find myself seizing up with the tension; I'd absolutely get the cramps and have to hand the tiller to Pod and just hobble around a bit to slacken off and I'd be right.

"The last race ended in a most extraordinary way. It looked for a bit as if McNamara could win it and beat us for the gold medal. We were leading, laying the windward end of the line in comfort, a quarter of a mile from the finish, abeam and to windward of McNamara and some other boats when we ran into this freak puff which put them all ahead. The boys had a look and said, 'Gee you're unlucky. They've tacked and they're going to cross us. Don't look, concentrate on your sailing, but we're gone'.

"But I couldn't resist it. I had a look and there was what I will never forget. McNamara was ahead of us alright, but to leeward of the Swede, Lars Thorn, who had won in Melbourne. And I thought, 'You've won yourself a gold medal. The bloke's gone a million; He's to leeward of the Swede who will take him right into that flag at the leeward end of the line. You've won a medal. It doesn't matter where we come.' And we just came about and went for the line. And sure enough, McNamara tacked and tried to clear the Swede's bow, but he had no hope. They hit and McNamara was disqualified."

Sturrock and Booth got their revenge on Northam in the Australian championship on Sydney Harbour, which followed the Games. "I told Bill, 'Norman Booth and Jock Sturrock are going to gang up on you just to say they have beaten the gold medallist,'" said Ingate. "He got beaten into third place behind Sturrock first and Booth second. I was fourth. And it was pathetic to watch; they ganged up on him and put him back, it was just terrible, just to say they could beat the gold medallist."

BARRANJOEY COULD HAVE been Ingate's. He had ordered the design from American Bill Luders in 1962. In his capacity as secretary of the 5.5 association Ingate went to see Northam, a prominent Sydney businessman as chairman of Johnson and Johnson, who was preparing to travel to the USA with Gretel's owner Sir Frank Packer, to watch the America's Cup. Northam was considering getting into the 5.5s for the 1964 Olympics.

Ingate suggested he see Bill Luders about a 5.5 design. "What are you going to do with the beautiful Caprice of Huon?" asked Ingate. Northam said he would sell it. "In a rush of blood to the stupid head I said, 'Would you sell it to me?' The deal was sealed over half a bottle of Johnny Walker Black Label whisky."

Ingate and his mother-in-law Nina Saalfeld bought the Robert Clark-design 46ft offshore racer from Northam. "Bill goes overseas, sees Bill Luders and gets the boat I had actually ordered," said Ingate. While Ingate campaigned Caprice of Huon offshore until 1972 he also continued to sail in the 5.5 class, buying Pam from Jock Sturrock's sponsor Otto Meik to contest the 1968 Olympic selection trials on Botany Bay. He lightened the hull by 36lb, added lead ballast, fitted an alloy boom and re-tuned the rig.

The trials ended sensationally with Bill Solomons skippering Bill Northam's 1964 gold medal winner Barranjoey to win on a tie-breaking placings countback from Norman Booth's new Olin Stephens design Southern Cross III with 29.7 points. Pam, with Ingate crewed by Ian Nathan and John Saalfeld, was third on 40.8 with 5-3-4-3-3-3-8 placings.

"At this stage I was getting all the best information I could on 5.5s as secretary of the association and passing it along to members and at one stage we had the strongest 5.5 class in the world," said Ingate.

Pam was third in the 1969 5.5 Gold Cup on Sydney Harbour won by Norm Booth's Southern Cross II from Tony Carr's vintage light weather flier Altair. The weather for the final heat was light, the type of breeze that Booth doesn't always enjoy. But Booth came out ahead of a match-race tacking duel to finish fifth, 49sec ahead of Altair.

Sailing with Booth were Bill Northam's 1964 Olympic gold medal crew Dick Sargeant and Peter O'Donnell. They sailed the Luders design

Southern Cross II in preference to the newer Sparkman and Stephens Southern Cross III, which was about to undergo underbody alterations allowed by recent changes to the class rules. Previous holder of the Cup Pam (Gordon Ingate) was third. "That's when we realised the Hunt boats were not as good as the Luders boats," Ingate said.

"NORMAN BOOTH WAS a competent sailor but from my point of view he was winning races by having the money. We were an amateur class, you never had to pay your crew, but Norman got over that by employing them in his car sales business: Carl Ryves, Pod O'Donnell, Dick Sargeant and if he said on a Tuesday, 'I am going out for a practice on the Dragon or the 5.5; put your sailing gear on we are going for a sail,' off they'd go. I got great pleasure when I could beat him. He was a millionaire, very successful in business. He had the time and he had the crew and it was nothing for them to go racing in America, Scandinavia, or Europe."

Booth was no late convert to sailing like Bill Northam. At the age of nine he built himself an 8ft canvas dinghy to race on the Lane Cove River. He went on to the 12ft Cadet dinghy training class, and was runner-up in the 1932 Stonehaven Cup Australian championship. He entered the Dragon class in the 1950s and with Adios won the Prince Philip Cup Australian championship in 1962. He began sailing 5.5s as well and in 1963 won the Australian championship with Southern Cross, a new design from American Ray Hunt built in Sydney by Billy Barnett, who crewed with Booth and Carl Ryves in the championship win.

"Why build a 5.5 when he was doing so well in Dragons?" Sheila Patrick asked Ingate in a Seacraft magazine interview. "I love racing boats. You only live once and though Dragons are wonderful, to be quite frank, limited in design and in the changes that can be made to the hull and the rigging. They were designed in 1928. The 5.5 is an open design and every year better hulls are being designed by the world's leading architects. The 5.5 is a 1963 boat and will always be completely the latest in everything. This I find very exciting and stimulating."

Ingate steered Pam to a hard-earned win in the 1969 Australian championship off Broken Bay to earn a trip to the world championship at Sandhamn, Sweden, later in the year. He almost invariably got good starts and even when buried managed to clear his air quickly, handled the shifts and tidal patterns well – significant after heavy rain the week before swelled the Hawkesbury River, which flows into Broken Bay. Mick Morris' spinnaker trimming was also an important part of Pam's improved showing in light weather. "We had waves coming aboard and I said to Mick, 'this is not salt water'; we were sailing in fresh water."

Although Ingate won three races, he had to fight to the last heat to beat Martin Visser, sailing Burrabra, who had scored three seconds. Visser was disqualified for being a premature starter in the last race. He protested Pam for failing to respond to a luff at the start. Ingate said that Pam could not respond because Carl Halvorsen's Crest, windward boat of the three, did not respond to his call for water. Visser's protest was eventually dismissed for not being lodged in time.

Tony Carr's Altair was third. Disappointment of the series was Norm Booth's new Sparkman & Stephens design Southern Cross III, the first 5.5 in the world to be fitted with a separate rudder on a skeg after a class rule change, which finished fifth. Australian 5.5 owners were the first in the world to sail with rudders hung separately from keels.

Later in 1969, Pam with Mick Morris and Ian Nathan crewing for Ingate, won the Scandinavian Gold Cup at Hanko, Norway. It was quite a pot; a heavy gold chalice of seashell design encrusted with diamonds and rubies. Ingate had to insure it for $150,000 before taking it to Australia. The Cup arouses fierce national rivalry and is given a great deal of newspaper space in the Scandinavian countries. It is sailed for on a sudden death knock-out basis. Each country is allowed only one entry and these go into a three-race elimination series. Only winners qualify for the final. Those three boats keep sailing until one has earned three wins over the whole series.

THE SYSTEM SUITED Ingate's aggressive starting tactics, the breezes tended to be fresh and crew and boat clicked with the help of a new-cut spinnaker with a flat circle of cloth in the head, developed by Borgen of Norway specially to suit the Gold Cup course which ends on a 60-degree triangle, with extremely shy reaches. "It was like a ballooner from the early 18-footers and 16-footers. The pole was always hard on the forestay," said Ingate.

In the first two qualifying races Pam did well on the wind but was murdered downwind by boats carrying Borgen spinnakers. Ingate managed to borrow one for the third race, which he won to qualify and went on to take the next two races to clinch the series. The other finalists were Fram IV (Crown Prince Harald of Norway) and Nemesis (Charlie Shumway, USA).

Surprisingly Sweden's Olympic gold medallists, the Sundelin brothers, didn't even qualify. Their Wasa IV was specifically designed for light breezes of Acapulco, the 1968 Olympic venue, which were never duplicated at Hanko. The seas were short and confused, something like the seas outside Broken Bay, where Ingate won the Australian championship.

Pam and crew went on to the 5.5 metre world championships at Sandhamn, an outer island of the Stockholm archipelago, Sweden, sailed in difficult conditions with big wind shifts in four of the seven races. Cybelle, sailed by Jean-Marie le Guillou of France, crewed by his brother Nicholas and Daniel Tassin, won with 3-1-6-6-3-1-1 placings for 23.1 points from Wasa IV (Jorgen Sundelin, Sweden), 15-3-1-1-4-4-5, 31.7 and Tomahawk (Thomas Nathhorst, Sweden), 1-8-4-3-11-3-3, 39.1.

Pam was the best of the three Australian boats competing, in seventh place with 9-5-9-7-6-5-9, 74.7. Crest (Carl Halvorsen) was tenth while Kings Cross (Frank Tolhurst) was just not at home in the lumpy, difficult seas and fresh winds.

Pam was as fast downwind as any – really fast under a spinnaker borrowed from Bill Northam – but lost ground upwind. The Ingate team did not navigate well in a couple of races where there were big shifts and over stood the weather mark. Ingate had the impression that the jib, which had been through three years of hard racing, was losing its punch (it was obviously fluttering) as the series went on. The Australians' show of strength with three entries helped secure the 1970 world championship for Sydney.

Pam, after winning the Australian championship, placed ninth with a scoreline of 7-dsq-4-9-7-9-11, in the world championship that followed off Broken Bay. The winner, steered by Dave Forbes, was Kevin McCann's Carabella, designed by Britton Chance for the 1968 Olympics, much improved by a new separate spade rudder, added after the rule change.

Nemesis (Ted Turner, USA) was second and Sundance (Ernie Fay, USA) third. Nemesis, one of the fastest boats, suffered from Ted's casual approach, particularly at the start of the series and a dismasting in the heat one resail. Then Turner got into the groove, won heats five and six, finished second to Carabella in heats four and seven, but it was too late. Crown Prince Harald of Norway was fourth sailing Carl Halvorsen's Luders design Quest.

Australian Gold Cup winner Southern Cross II (Norman Booth) was fifth. After making a promising start to the series by taking the stormy 30 knot heat one resail she slumped in the light-moderate air races and was unlucky in the last heat when she broke her boom just as she hit the lead after the second work. Her crew triced the broken pieces together by lashing the spare spinnaker pole along them, but she fell back to fifth place.

"We were sailing out at sea and always pretty rough offshore and a long way to sail from the Royal Prince Alfred Yacht Club at Green Point way out to the start line and all the way back made it a very long series and long hard days," said Ingate.

There were 18 starters in the series including six from overseas. Sweden's Tomatoe (Tom Nathhorst) finished sixth and gold medallist Peter Sundelin (Sweden) flew out at the last minute to take the helm of Baragoola, a Sydney boat owned by Russell Slade, of similar Chance design to Carabella and finished tenth.

Nemesis won the Scandinavian Gold Cup, which preceded the worlds, in a tension-packed final series from John B (Bobby Symonette, Bahamas) and Tomatoe. Turner missed the first two qualifying heats of the Gold Cup so that he could sail his converted Twelve Metre American Eagle in a Southern Ocean Racing conference race. Ernie Fay sailed the boat without success in the first two qualifying races, won by Tomatoe and John B.

Then Turner jetted into Sydney on the morning of the third heat, grabbed a cab for Pittwater, took the helm of Nemesis and won the race. The three winners then had to race on until one had three wins. John B won the next race, gaining the jump at the start in a light breeze from Turner, who started badly. Turner settled in to win the next two races, the last by 20sec from Tomatoe, having disposed of John B by close covering early in the race. The margins in all races were extremely close, usually less than a minute, despite the differences in design.

Southern Cross II (Norm Booth) won the Australian Gold Cup, which opened the world championship regatta on Sydney Harbour through the usual 'steeplechase' hazards of commercial shipping and ferries. The big surprise of the series was the fine showing of Sydney skiff sailor Ken Beashel at the helm of the Bahamian yacht John B. Beashel sailed skilfully and in daredevil fashion across the bows of ferries and under the sterns of ships, to steer John B into second place.

Norm Booth, crewed by Peter O'Donnell and Dick Sargeant, sailed a steady series, topped off by two consecutive wins by good starting tactics and speed in the fresh breeze he likes best. Booth then had to withdraw from the final heat after being caught with nowhere to go by John

B on starboard, going through a bunch of downwind boats converging on the mark. If Tomatoe, at that stage placed second to Carabella, held her place to the finish she would have won the Cup. But in an exciting last work, Beashel gained a slight edge and then an outgoing ship's wash threw Tomatoe crewman Claes Botje overboard. In the confusion of retrieving him, Tomatoe was caught port-and-starboard by Barranjoey (Brian Northam) and retired.

Ingate has fond memories of the characters in the class at that time, headed by Ted Turner, the loud and fast talker from America's South: "We were at a black-tie dinner at the Royal Sydney Yacht Squadron, said Ingate. "Ted wasn't a good drinker by any means. He was sitting at the top of the table saying how much he enjoyed coming to Australia and being with Australians. 'I just love it so much' and he slipped out of his chair and slid under the table. The head waiter came over and said, 'Mr Ingate, we can't have your friend going to sleep on the floor of the Royal Sydney Yacht Squadron' and I said, 'Ted, you've got to get up,' and he said, 'Ah, I am enjoying myself, it's lovely.'"

He also remembers Turner's introduction of Crown Prince Harald of Norway to a group of sailors and journalists sitting around in the Royal Prince Alfred clubhouse over a beer at the 1970 worlds, waiting for results, when Ted Turner joined them and immediately had them in stitches with his review of the day's racing and wondering aloud (loudly) of what he could do with the 20 or so bags of sails that had been shipped to Australia with his boat. A quiet, shy young man joined the group – Crown Prince Harald of Norway. While the assembly didn't know whether to stand, bow or shake hands, Ted fixed it all up with a "this is the Prince, hi Prince", sort of introduction and the conversation and drinking went comfortably on.

Frank Tolhurst / INGATE FAMILY ARCHIVE

Ingate first met Crown Prince Harald and Princess Sonja at the 1969 Scandinavian Gold Cup in Hanko where the princess was presented with the very first Yngling. "She was a good sailor, going out for a sail in the Yngling and she asked me to crew for her. I sailed with her as forward hand for the day and it was great fun; we got on really well and I gave her a great hug as we came ashore, a moment a photographer captured, with Prince Harald in the background, which ended up on the front page of a newspaper."

Also remembered fondly is Sydney skipper Frank Tolhurst who won the world championship three times (1976, 1978, 1979), the Scandinavian Gold Cup four times and the Australian championship five times and branched into E22s just long enough to win an Etchells world championship on Royal Prince Alfred YC's Palm Beach course in 1978.

Bobby Symonette / BOB ROSS

TOLHURST SAID, AFTER he was beaten into second place with Arunga III by the Bahamian veteran Bobby Symonette sailing John B, in 1980: "This latest world series was excellent. It proved once again that although the fives are one-off boats, the difference in boat speed is certainly not tremendous. The different designs have an edge in their favoured conditions and you still have to have a good all-round boat.

"The 5.5s are tremendous boats to race to windward. Etchells and Solings are lighter, accelerate very quickly and you can win or lose more places on just one puff of wind or one very slight shift where the fives are really tactical. You need to give a lot more thought to the tactics you apply and particularly to your competitors. That's the sort of racing I really enjoy and that is why I am a dedicated 5.5 racer, particularly in international competition, they are really a fine bunch of guys who appreciate close racing. They certainly claim any advantage they have by the rules, strictly sail to them, but do not try to bend the rules with unnecessary protests. And this is what really makes the competition so good and has certainly encouraged us to go back time and time again to race overseas.

"The difference between stop and go in tuning a five is very little. The adjustments that are necessary are fine but generally, once you have them set up and going they are not finicky boats, they don't go in and out of tune. A characteristic of the class is that the five will point high and continue to point high, although this depends on the gear you are using, the sea condition and the velocity of the wind. You can make some other boats climb but unless you come off quickly you will stall them out. You can certainly stall a five but, with their higher ballast ratio, they tend to go higher longer."

Frank's success in fives was heavily due to his ability to organise good boats and good crew. If he could not get a competent crew for an event he would not race. Boatbuilder Keith Ravell was with him from the start of his career in fives, 'shanghaied' while he was building a Cherub for Frank's son Mark. Mark and Norm Hyett sailed with Frank in his 1976 world championship win and John Stanley in the 1978 Etchells win.

Ingate remembers Bobby Symonette as another stalwart of the class. Symonette, a successful businessman, member of a prominent Bahamian political family who served as Speaker of the Bahamas' House of Assembly, represented the Bahamas in 5.5s at five Olympic Games: Melbourne (1956), Rome (1960), Tokyo (1964), Acapulco (1968) in 5.5s and Munich (1972) in the Soling class. Symonette twice won the 5.5 metre world championship in Sydney, in 1980 and 1986.

IN THE 1986 win, Symonette, crewed by John Rumsey and Robert Penticoff, sailed John B VIII. Helena (Tom Jungell, Finland), pre-series favourite after comfortably winning the Australian championship, was second, Busy B (Jan Erik Dyvi, Norway) third. Jan IV (Bruce Ritchie, Aus) won the Scandinavian Gold Cup.

Symonette was also a strong contributor to the administration of the sport, serving as president of the International 5.5 Metre Class Association for many years, as an International Yacht Racing Union judge and president of the Bahamas Olympic Association from 1957 to 1972.

He started sailing as an 11-year-old in the Bahamas, went offshore racing for a while, with notable experiences crewing on Finisterre, Carleton Mitchell's Sparkman & Stephens 38ft centreboard yawl design that won the Newport-Bermuda race three times and was on Huey Long's Ondine, when took line honours in the 1962 Sydney-Hobart race. "I met him in 1972 when I did my first Hobart race with Caprice of Huon and was associated with him in the 5.5s right up until the time he died (in March 1998)," said Ingate. "He was great contributor to international yachting. He was a fun guy, too; a bit of a mischief maker."

Ingate took a break from the 5.5s from 1969 to concentrate on racing Caprice of Huon and to campaign in the Tempest class later in 1969

1981 world championship, Nassau. Winner Rhapsody (Roy Tutty, Australia) chasing Pop's John B (Bobby Symonette) / AUSTRALIAN SAILING ARCHIVE

towards selection in the 1972 and 1976 Olympics. He sold Pam in 1973 but continued to retain an interest in the class, which remained strong with new boats in Sydney as well as in Europe and the USA and some good results. Roy Tutty's Rhapsody from Royal Prince Alfred Yacht Club, with Tutty crewed by Colin Beashel and Phil Smidmore, won the 1981 world championship at Nassau in the Bahamas with Frank Tolhurst's Arunga III second. Rhapsody was a Bill Luders design built by Neville Fisher at RPAYC in cold-moulded Honduras mahogany.

FRANK TOLHURST'S ARUNGA IV, designed by Australians Warren Muir and Ben Lexcen and built in cold-moulded wooden laminate by Keith Ravell, sold on to American Al Cassel in 1980, became the mould form for the first series of economically-priced fibreglass 5.5s built in the USA by the Melges Boat Works with the first one delivered to Bob Mosbacher in 1985.

In 1990, to counter the trend towards one-design by the Melges boats, Sydney businessman Colin Ryan, who was the International Vice President of the 5.5 Metre class and Frank Tolhurst, who both had Melges boats, decided to have their own limited run of 5.5s built by Andrew Hudson at Careening Cove on Sydney Harbour, to lines originally drawn by Ben Lexcen, modified by his partner Peter Lowe of Lexcen, Lowe Yacht Design.

Hudson, who had just built the original Lexcen design Trilogy, in cold-laminated mahogany for the trilogy of himself, Michael Lee and Jack Christoffersen, built six fibreglass sister-ships in a row off the mould from 1991: Arunga X for Frank Tolhurst, Sic Em Rex for Colin Ryan, John B VIII for Bobby Symonette, Carmen for Vladimir Marschan (Finland), Salamander IV for Jonathan Janson (GBR) and Lovana II (Hans-Jürgen Quiesser, Germany). Colin Ryan in 1994 had had Hudson build him Sic Em Rex II to a design modified from the original by Iain Murray.

Ingate had tried to buy Trilogy. "She was the most beautiful-looking boat, designed by Ben, but I was a little bit slow off the mark and it went to a bloke up in Brisbane."

He returned to serious 5.5 racing when, with owner Colin Ryan unavailable, he skippered Ryan's Sic Em Rex II, crewed by Ryan's son Mark and Chris Hutchison, in the 1998 world championship sailed from the Royal Corinthian Yacht Club at Cowes. He was inspired to return to the class by the presence of former friends in it, including Jonathan Janson who he had first met at the 1956 Prince Philip Cup for the Dragon class in Melbourne. Janson was sailing mainsheet hand for Graham Mann, skippering the Duke of Edinburgh's Bluebottle, which had won the bronze medal in the Olympics, which immediately preceded the Prince Philip Cup.

The winner in Cowes was Glen Foster, a New York stockbroker, sailing the 1993 Doug Peterson-designed, Melges Boat Works-built My Shout. Ingate had become close friends with Foster during his 1972 Olympic campaign. Foster won the bronze medal in Tempests at the 1972 Games.

Foster named his 5.5 My Shout because he had been mystified by the Australians' frequent call on the Tempest campaigns at the bar after racing: "It's your shout Glenn."

"'Why would I want to shout?' he'd reply," said Ingate

Foster, died in 1999, aged 69 of oesophageal cancer, just 14 days after returning home from winning the Scandinavian Gold Cup and placing third in the world championship on Lake Garda, Italy, where Ingate sailed the Elvin Still (Finland) design Addam Addam into 18th place. Foster with My Shout had won three world championships (1995, 1997, 1998) and three Scandinavian Gold Cups (1996, 1998, 1999).

Ingate continued to sail Addam Addam in the world and European events through 1999 and 2000 and 2001. Crewed by David Ellis and James Bevis he was sixth in a fleet of 38 at the 2001 worlds in Flensburg, Germany. "After the 2001 worlds, two young guys who were there approached me with an offer to buy Addam Addam, so I was able to sell it to them and approach Glen's son Colin with an offer to sell My Shout to me after Colin had skippered her to 11th place."

Colin Foster sold the boat to Ingate who later in 2001 entered the 5.5m class at Kiel Week for his most memorable win in the class, at the age of 75, crewed by David Ellis and James Bevis. My Shout won five of the seven races in a fleet of 16.

"In those years, Kiel Week was the biggest regatta in the world with something like 5,000 yachts. We won five races of the seven and were named winner of Kiel Week for being the winner of most races in our division. The reaction was completely unexpected; to be surrounded by the media – they thought it was marvellous – and here's me in headlines in German, 'The King of Kiel' and on TV. The places we went to and the people we met; it was a lot of fun. Kiel Week just showed what a good boat My Shout was and we had a great crew."

JOINING INGATE ON his travels was Margaret Hearder, the widow of Sydney photographer John Hearder, who died in 2000. Ingate, whose wife Sally had died in 1998 had been a friend of Margaret since the 1950s. "I met Margaret when she was 17," he said. She married John a year later. Before John passed away in 2000 he told me, 'It's your turn to look after her'. Their relationship continued happily until Margaret died in 2015.

German band entertains at Flensburg during the Scandinavian Gold Cup, 2001
INGATE FAMILY ARCHIVE

My Shout in a runaway win at the 2001 Kiel Week regatta / INGATE FAMILY ARCHIVE

My Shout at Kiel Week
INGATE FAMILY ARCHIVE

In 2002, My Shout won the Finnish open championship and was fourth in the world championship that followed in Helsinki. Ingate continued to campaign My Shout in Europe each year and in Bermuda in 2008, until he sold her in 2009. He brought her to Australia only in 2004-2005 for the Australian championship (second), Scandinavian Gold Cup (sixth) and world championship (eighth).

MY SHOUT, WITH Neville Wittey and Tony Hearder crewing for Ingate, made a great start to the 2005 world championship on Sydney Harbour with a third and a win in the first two races. But she was disqualified from race three after colliding with Addam Cubed (Jussi Gulichsen, Finland) on the starting line and eventually finished eighth overall with 3-1-dsq-9-6-9-11-10-7-8-13 placings. Three-times Olympic gold medallist Jochen Schümann of Germany, in a polished crew combination with Ronald Pieper and Peter van Niekerk, won without having to start in the last race.

Ingate explained the collision: "A third boat was involved and ducking

Margaret Hearder and Gordon, happy at Kiel Week / INGATE FAMILY ARCHIVE

Ingate at Kiel Week INGATE FAMILY ARCHIVE

him put me into collision with Gulichsen. I had no alternative but to protest the third boat. I was on starboard, he was on port and to miss him I hit Gulichsen."

He was critical of the race management team: "The whole series was sailed in sou'easters with the starts in Taylor Bay, windward marks in Rose Bay, across the ferry lanes. We started at one o'clock and the

Kiel Week presentation: Gordon flanked by crewmen David Ellis (left) and James Beavis / INGATE FAMILY ARCHIVE

Bowman Nev Wittey in a spinnaker drop, 2005 worlds / BOB ROSS

starter would not alter the start time, although when we had a ferry coming from Circular Quay and a ferry coming from Manly at the same time that he got us under way. It was absolutely pathetic; that's my eighth place."

My Shout (AUS 82) well positioned in a start, 2005 worlds / BOB ROSS

Running out of Rose Bay, 2005 worlds / BOB ROSS

My Shout in the 2005 worlds on Sydney Harbour / BOB ROSS

6

OFFSHORE WITH CAPRICE OF HUON

ALTHOUGH HE PREFERS INSHORE RACING around the buoys in one-design keelboats, offshore racing gave Gordon Ingate his greatest success internationally. His pre-World War II designed 45-footer Caprice of Huon top scored in the 1965 Admiral's Cup international teams series for offshore racers, then sailed every second year from Cowes, Isle of Wight, UK.

She won the first three races and the Australian team went into the fifth triple-scoring last race of the series, the 605n mile Fastnet race, only 14 points behind the British team. Caprice rounded the Fastnet rock ahead of her British rivals. The home team however, then gained a winning break by sailing into the Atlantic while the Australians stood west into the Irish Sea, chasing a forecast wind swing. Instead, the wind moved back to into the south-east, giving the British yachts a fast free-sheet course for the leg back to the finish in Plymouth.

Two years later Caprice, skippered by Gordon Reynolds with Ingate committed to an America's Cup program was, with Ted Kaufman's Mercedes III and Robert Crichton-Brown's Balandra, a member of the Australian team that won the Admiral's Cup.

Ingate continued racing Caprice of Huon when he could, between campaigning for the America's Cup, Olympic 5.5, Tempest and Star classes. She placed second in the 1972 Sydney-Hobart race to Ted Turner's American Eagle. Ingate had a very personal affection for Caprice among all the boats he has owned: "I don't cry very often but I was very upset by selling Caprice in 1975 because I was getting involved in the America's Cup with Gretel II. It was a great boat."

CAPRICE OF HUON'S fine lines came from the board of British designer Robert Clark before World War Two, commissioned by Tasmanian apple grower Charles Calvert. The main Huon Pine timbers were cut when war broke out and the build was shelved. In 1949 Calvert had the original timbers taken out of storage and 70-year-old shipwright Vivian Innes, working alone, took three years to complete building Caprice.

Ingate marvelled at the methods Innes used. After each Hobart race with Caprice, Ingate would visit the Calvert family at Waterloo Bay, around the corner from Port Cygnet on the Huon River. "The boat was designed to race against the Eight-Metre yachts racing in Hobart, Siandra (Max Creese) and Norske (Charles Davies) and used to beat them. During a visit to the Calverts, Ingate met Viv Innes. "He was a great old bloke."

Inglis built the boat in a cow shed on the shores of the bay. "In preparation for the launching in 1951, he was able turn it at right angles and position it for launching all on his own," said Ingate. Realising that the tide would not be right for the hull to clear the shore-side rock face on the nominated official launching day, Innes launched the boat on his own, with no onlookers. With two four-inch piles

The cowshed where Caprice of Huon was built, her builders' frames still resting against it, in 1964 / GORDON INGATE

holding up the hull, he knocked the chocks out and Caprice slid down into the water. He told Ingate: "She bounced over the rock into deep water. If I had waited for people to come down, the tide would have been too low and she would have done a nasty job on the rock."

Innes showed Ingate the ingenious device he developed to fasten Caprice's hull planks with copper nails and roves. "It was like a huge horseshoe with a single bolt on a dolly that he would slide around the horseshoe shape and fit on the head of the nail. He would then go inside the boat, put the rove on the nail and by pulling on a string push against the nail and rivet the head over. That's how he built the boat on his own, complaining bitterly that the copper nails he was using weren't as good as they were 50 years ago. All the gold had been taken out of the copper; it was too refined. In the old days the gold in the copper made it hard and it was much tighter to rivet."

Ingate first got to know Bill Northam, who was to buy Caprice from the Calverts in 1957, when Northam began sailing his first yacht, Gymea, in the 1950s. Northam, a successful Sydney businessman did not take up sailing until he was 46. On being taken for a sail by a neighbour on Pittwater, Northam found he had a real feel on the helm, which he attributed to racing cars on dirt tracks in his younger days. He bought a veteran Sydney-Hobart racer Gymea and began to race her, undeterred by disqualification from his first race for hitting the start boat. Ingate recalls sailing with Northam on Gymea when they messed up a start on the Royal Sydney Yacht Squadron's Saturday start line. "How do I start?" said Northam.

"I said, 'We are going to start on starboard.' The bloke on the mainsheet pulled it on and we were going to be too early. 'Stop the boat,'" Ingate said.

"'How do I do that?'

"'Push the helm down.'

"He pushed it too far and we went aback. I pulled the helm the other way, we stopped on the start line and went backwards. I said 'Bill, I have never sailed backwards off a start line'; anyway, we joked about it."

Northam's next boat was the Eight Metre Saskia, designed and built by William Fife, the legendary Scot. Saskia, representing Royal Sydney Yacht Squadron, won the Sayonara Cup interclub club challenge match in 1955, winning three out of the four races from the defender Frances (Ernie Digby, Royal Yacht Club of Victoria) and Tasmanian challenger Erica J (Ted Domeney).

Caprice with cut-down mast in 1962, painted by Jack Earl / GORDON INGATE

Caprice was dismasted soon after the start of the 1957 Sydney-Hobart race. She placed fourth in 1958 after being becalmed in Storm Bay when Northam reckoned she was in a winning position.

Ingate bought her in July 1962 when he visited Northam, who was about to depart to watch the 1962 America's Cup in Newport with his friend, Sir Frank Packer, head of the Gretel challenger syndicate. In his capacity as secretary of the Australian 5.5 Metre Association, Ingate asked Northam to visit the American designer/builder Bill Luders to check on the progress of the new 5.5 Ingate had ordered. Northam commented: "You know Gordon, I would be happier in a smaller boat. I think I will get into the 5.5s."

"You're joking Bill, you've got that beautiful boat Caprice; what are you going to do with it?"

"'I think I will sell it.'

"You really want to sell Caprice of Huon? And he said 'yeah'.

"And I said, 'Gee Bill I would love to be able to buy it.'

"He reached into the bottom drawer and out came a bottle of Johnny Walker and he said, 'Let's have a talk about this Gordon.' This was about 11 o'clock in the morning; by 12 o'clock I'd bought it. It was very cheap;

Caprice in the 1963 Hobart, closing the Tasmanian coast / GORDON INGATE

it was an impressive boat; he had a paid hand working on it full time; it was very well looked after, had perfect varnish and paint jobs but there were a lot of things wrong with it.

"And he said, 'Okay, I will pick up your 5.5.' That was the boat that became Barranjoey, a real part of history and I got Caprice of Huon. Bill wasn't an ocean racer. He liked Saskia, which he bought after his first boat, because he knew nothing about sailing."

When Ingate bought Caprice of Huon, he said it was a very slow boat. "Bill replaced the lovely spruce mast that had been in the boat and not knowing any better said to Alan Payne, 'design me a mast that will not break'; the worst thing you could say to Alan Payne.

"When we sailed on the harbour she was on her ear all the time; she was impossible to control. That wooden mast was enormous. So, the first thing I did was get the boys to put me up the mast in a bosun's chair.

I had a hand saw and I cut seven feet off the top of the mast for a loss of 13sq metres of sail area; it was crazy. The boat suddenly came alive; I could steer it and the rating came down dramatically."

IN HER FIRST season before the alteration, Caprice did win the Royal Sydney Yacht Squadron's traditional Gascoigne Cup day race over an approximately 30n mile course after surviving an edge-of-control incident that could have knocked her out of the race. Sheila Patrick wrote in Seacraft: "After an exciting tack-for-tack match race with Dick Dickson's Eight Metre Norske, which was forced to retire half-way through the race with a broken cross-tree, Gordon was busy gybing Caprice as they entered the Heads, running before a fresh nor'-easter, when for'ard hand Neil Bennett, who is only slight, left the deck, clinging like a silkworm to the spinnaker pole as it skied 15ft into the air. The

Ted Butler steering and Lloyd Sustenance on watch, 1963 Sydney–Hobart / GORDON INGATE

crew held their breath as Neil, clinging tightly to the pole, waved about in the sky for an endless minute and then arrived safely on deck. The spinnaker didn't even spill a drop of wind and the gybe continued perfectly."

Caprice was ninth to finish and 25th on handicap in the 1962 Sydney-Hobart race. New York shipowner Sumner A. (Huey) Long's 57ft aluminium yawl Ondine set a new race record of three

Gordon Ingate eating, Sydney–Hobart 1963
INGATE FAMILY ARCHIVE

days 3hr 46min 16sec in taking line honours in conditions that suited two-masted boats: south-easterly of 18-20 knots at the start backing to the east and freshening to 25 knots. During the next two days, the fleet of 42 continued to enjoy fast reaching and running with the wind backing to the north-east and remaining fresh until it died off the Tasmanian coast.

Caprice was among the fleet leaders in the 1963 Hobart race after light and variable winds scrambled placings on the first three days. With hardly any wind on the morning of day four she was grouped off Eddystone Point on the north-east coast of Tasmania, with Norm Brooker's new Sparkman & Stephens 43ft sloop Sea Wind and Trygve and Magnus Halvorsen's 38ft double ender Freya. With a strong south-west change forecast, they were converging on the coast.

The promised sou'-wester developed on day five, with the wind freshening firstly from the north-west. Astor, laying Tasman Island with sprung sheets, quickly scorched through to the lead, with the wind up to 40 knots and extremely cold. She rounded Tasman with three reefs in the main and small jib to finish first at 21.53 on December 30.

The boats that followed had a progressively tougher time with the sou-'wester lasting 48 hours with 60-65 knots of wind and gusts of up to 70 knots reported in Storm Bay. The sturdy Freya finished second, four hours, 24 minutes behind Astor to win the race on corrected time by two hours and two seconds from Lal McDonnell's new Carmen class 30-footer Cavalier with Norman Rydge's new Payne-designed masthead sloop Lorita Maria third.

CAPRICE WAS FOURTH to finish and ninth on handicap. "We had incredibly close racing with Norm Brooker's new S&S 43-footer Sea Wind, which finished third across the line," said Ingate. Caprice laid into Tasman Island under mainsail only. "It was blowing so hard," said Ingate. "And it was so cold as we turned the corner, we had icicles on the rigging; I was wiping them off with my hand and there was snow on Mount Wellington – in the middle of summer."

Freya's win, the first of a record-breaking three consecutive wins in the Hobart, was remarkable for a small boat in those conditions, said Ingate. "The biggest thing I learned about ocean racing came from the Halvorsens and their long-time crewman Trevor Gowland: if the race is more than 200n miles, you never ever went hard on the wind; you always sailed the boat as fast as you could. You get to the next shift first and tack. The moment we went out the Heads, we just sailed free."

Over a few beers in a dockside pub after the race the move began to test the quality of the Australian offshore fleet against the best in the world. Trygve Halvorsen, Norman Rydge, whose Alan Payne-designed 39-footer Lorita Maria had finished third and CYCA Commodore Bill Psaltis who had finished 18th in his ageing Lass 'O Luss decided on the suggestion of Commodore Psaltis to investigate sending a team to the Admiral's Cup international teams series for offshore yachts, sailed biennially in conjunction with the Cowes Week regatta in England. "The best of the rest of the world was then the Admiral's Cup," said Psaltis. "Norman and Tryg had decided they were going to England anyway for the Fastnet race and Cowes Week."

The Admiral's Cup from 1957 was initially sailed within regular events raced from Cowes: The Channel race (about 225n miles to the coast of France and back); Britannia Cup and New York Yacht Club Cup day races of about 30n miles on The Solent within Cowes Week and the Fastnet race (about 605n miles) from Cowes, around Fastnet Rock off the south-eastern corner of Ireland and back to finish at Portsmouth. By 1965 it had broadened from an inaugural Great Britain-USA challenge to a truly international series for teams of three yachts.

Early in 1964 a committee was formed, chaired by Sir James Kirby and with CYCA secretary Merv Davey joining Halvorsen, Rydge and Psaltis, which organised funding for the venture. Qantas would provide air travel, P&O would carry the yachts to Europe and back, Rothmans Australia Ltd agreed to be a sponsor. The estimated $15,000 accommodation cost in England would be raised by club and crew fund-raising events. The CYCA's board accepted the committee's proposal and advised yacht clubs throughout Australia that a series of evaluation races would be held late in 1964 to select the team.

Ingate decided to enter the trials and began recruiting crew and optimising Caprice in his trademark meticulous manner. First to join, in 1964, was an old friend Graham Newland, who was to make a significant contribution to optimising the hull and rig. They had known each other since school days at Sydney Technical High School, where Newland had been a good footballer and swimmer in GPS sports. Ingate introduced Newland to sailing when Newland was about 27. Their families had been closely associated since World War One when their fathers had served overseas together. Graham grew up with Gordon's elder brother Jack and one day Gordon invite Graham to go for a sail.

"I was concerned that Graham was going downhill," said Ingate. "He was going the wrong way, spending his Saturdays playing billiards and betting on horses." Ingate invited him to come sailing on Jasnar one Saturday afternoon in the Cruising Yacht Club of Australia's Coogee and return race. "He said, 'How long has this been going on?' He enjoyed every minute and in no time at all I got him out of his rut. Within three months, he had bought his own boat, a 28ft straight stemmer called Firefly, which was a wreck. But he was a clever engineer and he had Firefly rebuilt. He spent a lot of time on Firefly. He cruised it a lot, sailed it to Port Stephens and the Myall River cruising up to Bulladelah in challenging shallow waters."

While Newland had Firefly up on the slips at Ford's Berry's Bay, to be re-timbered and have new keel bolts fitted, he met boatbuilder Ron Swanson, who was building himself an 18-footer. When Newland decided to go for a better boat and chose the Arthur Robb Lion Class design 35-footer Siandra, he employed Ron Swanson on wages to build it.

Siandra, with a strong crew including Swanson and thorough boat preparation and crew-training program, won the Sydney-Hobart race in 1958 and 1960. Making fittings for Siandra gradually led the Newland engineering business into specialising in yacht hardware. Newland joined Ingate again on Caprice of Huon, making a valuable contribution to refining the rig, hull and handicap rating before making a career from helping set up new ocean racers including Syd Fischer's Sparkman & Stephens 48-footer and Arthur Byrne's near sister ship Salacia II. He became the American S&S design firm's personal representative in Australia.

Newland, with sailmaker Peter Cole who was just branching into supplying spars, designed a new aluminium mast for Caprice in 1963. "It was the same length as the wooden spar that took ten people to lift and two of us could lift it and suddenly Caprice became a champion", said Ingate. Newland worked on reducing Caprice's handicap rating.

"'The name of the game is handicap' Graham used to say. Forget speed, you've got to get the boat sailing to its handicap.' And that's what we did; from the bottom of the boat to the top of the mast, every single measurement he took to the nth degree, down to an eighth of an inch, to take the rating down."

The biggest single improvement Newland made was to streamline the propeller aperture in the keel. "We were sailing along one day and he said, 'Gordon, there is something wrong with the stern of this boat;

there's too much water coming out to windward.' Next time we slipped the boat we had a look. 'The propeller aperture is much too big,' Graham said. 'The boat's making leeway and the water is coming down the leeward side and up through the aperture.' Graham suggested that we should replace the three-bladed propeller with a two-blade, stand it up in the aperture and close the aperture right up. He designed the aperture to follow the shape of the propeller so that even with the propeller upright there was very little water coming through the aperture. The propeller was big enough for the boat to do the six knots under the rule that applied in 1963 and the rating came down.

"Everything Graham did on Caprice was to bring the rating down. We didn't even have a block at the top of the mast for the spinnaker halyard. The halyard just went through a hole in an aluminium casting so we had maximum spinnaker area. And we started to win race after race. Graham went from being an absolute scallywag in Chatswood to becoming a legend in his own time as a yacht master."

Recruited navigator Bill Fesq was to become the most invaluable member of the crew at the Admiral's Cup for his knowledge of British waters from the time he spent serving on small ships with Royal Navy in World War Two and for his studies of the working model of the Solent's tricky tidal flows at Southampton University just before the Cup.

Another top-quality recruit was foredeck hand Mick York, a marine engineer, who had been a forward hand on Australia's first America's Cup challenger, Gretel, in 1962. "He was a very good crew, self-taught to a large extent, who had done his time as crew aboard a steamer so his knowledge of anything to do with the water was absolutely excellent," said Ingate. "He became responsible for getting the crewing techniques worked up so we were making the minimum of mistakes. Mick had navigating skills and his seamanship was second to none."

Ingate's crew learned from York's experience aboard Gretel about reducing windage, so all the halyards when not in use, were moused (replaced by a loop of light cordage through the mast) lifebuoys were laid flat or over the stern and the crew lay flat on deck when going upwind. "It made a tremendous difference," said Ingate. To demonstrate the effect of windage to his crew in training Ingate used to carry a 12-inch square of Masonite and get crewmen to hold it up to windward. "They could hardly hold it and I would say, 'That's what your body is doing in terms of windage.'"

Backing up on the foredeck was Fred Thomas ('Fearless Fred') who began his offshore career as a teenager, crewing on Sir Claude Plowman's Morna and was taught a great deal by Ron Robertson, the skipper and Sydney's best forward hand in big boats, Ronald ('Rubber') Kellaway. "Fred became quite knowledgeable in the art of sailing big boats and wasn't fazed handling gear in difficult heavy weather conditions," said Ingate. "He was quite valuable in telling us how to do things but in a way that always had a joke attached to it so it remained part of the fundamental good regime that existed on Caprice of Huon. It was a very happy crew from the time we started. If we did have a bit of a downturn, the enthusiasm of the crew generally pulled us back up."

Gordon Reynolds, alternate helmsman, was introduced to Ingate by Graham Newland through his association with Middle Harbour Yacht Club, where he had learned his sailing on Eudoria, owned by his brother-in-law Norman Way. "I said to Graham, 'we need another helmsman to stand one of the watches, so everyone could rest, because I didn't intend to stand a watch'" said Ingate. "I took the role of being the skipper, on call at any time; same with the navigator Bill Fesq. The way we set the watches up there could always be a change of sail; the words 'all hands on deck' were never used. We tried not to have any emergencies. Change of sail or gybing was done with the minimum of crew, not the maximum.' Reynolds was to skipper Caprice of Huon in the Australian team that won the 1967 Admiral's Cup, in the absence of Ingate who was campaigning Gretel II towards an America's Cup challenge.

Dr John Saalfeld, Ingate's brother-in-law, was the "junior midshipman of the crew," said Ingate. "He was fantastic. Being a medical man, he became in charge of our well-being and he was in charge of doing any of the jobs any of us would not take on. But he enjoyed it."

New sails were added to the wardrobe by Sydney sailmaker Joe Pearce who had recently acquired the Hood cloth franchise. "Joe Pearce had just come back from America. Ted Hood had taken a liking to Joe and taught him practically everything he knew," said Ingate. "Joe built us a 100 per cent (foretriangle) number two headsail and it was so good, we used it when we should have had a big headsail on and also in winds up to 35 knots. It was an ideal sail for flat water. We used it when it was blowing pretty hard in the selection trials for the Admiral's Cup team and we used that headsail a lot in the Solent during the Admiral's Cup in flat water and a lot of wind. Joe then made us a new mainsail, number three headsail and two new spinnakers."

The Australian team selection trials series comprised the 350n mile

Caprice (13) trailing Camille (Swanson brothers) and overlapped with Mercedes II (Ted Kaufman) in the Admiral's Cup trials, 1964 / INGATE FAMILY ARCHIVE

Montagu Island race, two 30n mile windward-return races off Sydney Heads and the 200n mile Cabbage Tree Island race. All were sailed in strong winds, which suited the double-enders Freya, the Halvorsen brothers' 38-footer and Ron Swanson's 36ft Camille, Swanson's development of the successful Wally Ward-designed Carmen class. Selection of the third team member came down to the Cabbage Tree Island race between Caprice and Arthur Byrne's new Sparkman & Stephens 41-footer Salacia.

THE CABBAGE TREE was sailed in a south-west gale that had Caprice in trouble on the leg from Sydney to Cabbage Tree. "We broached a couple of times very badly," said Ingate. "So much so that the spinnaker wrapped itself around the forestay. Mick York and I went up the forestay, using snatch blocks, to the top and started to cut the spinnaker away. As we cut down the forestay we found our knives would last literally maybe five minutes so we rigged up a system to lower our knives to Gordon Reynolds, who sharpened the knives and sent them up again. It took us probably two hours to get the spinnaker down. Mick and I were not feeling too well when we came down.

"We set another spinnaker, a storm spinnaker. What we didn't know was that Salacia was also having trouble. We came around the island and started to beat back. The starboard lower crosstree fell out. I had to go up the mast and put it back in. We were heading inshore on port tack and I thought, cripes, if I don't get it fixed, we won't be able to tack and will be out of the race. We beat Salacia II home by about an hour. When they finally calculated the points for the series, we had beaten Salacia by one point.

A strong push developed at the club (Cruising Yacht Club of Australia) that because Salacia was a brand-new boat and Caprice was 13 years old, Salacia should be chosen over Caprice. However, Merv Davey, CYCA secretary who was also secretary of the Admiral's Cup selection committee, maintained that the race instructions said the boats would be chosen on points and the chairman of the selection committee, Ray Kirby, took the same view. There was also a move to ban Caprice crewman Fred Thomas, a blunt talker, from the team. "I said Fred was part of the winning team and if he wasn't going, we weren't going," said Ingate. "His input was excellent; he was a very knowledgeable ocean racing guy, brought up on Morna as a youngster in the early Hobart racing."

The three crews quickly formed a strong team spirit and became close knit before leaving Australia. They trained together in Broken Bay to become used to racing in tidal current flow. "The Hawkesbury wasn't a patch on The Solent," said Ingate.

Before the team was shipped to England, Caprice fitted the first set of winches made by Malcolm Barlow, a toolmaker working in a garage in Bondi on the way to establishing a very successful, internationally-marketed range. "They were far ahead of any others," said Ingate. "We could out tack the other boats because those winches were just so good."

Ingate revealed that Barlow had copied the American Barient winch designed by Tim Mosely, who had been an engineer with Boeing and a sailor at St Francis Yacht Club, San Francisco. "Top boats at the club were the 72ft yawl Baruna and 63ft cutter Orient. Tim told their owners, 'Your winches are bloody awful', went back to Boeing and used its technology to design the winches for Barient, a combination of the names of those two boats. Malcolm Barlow was worried on learning that Mosely was going to visit Australia because he had copied the Barient winch perfectly. I had got friendly with him at St Francis and I invited him down to Caprice of Huon.

"He said, 'You've got some of my winches.'

"No Tim, they're not yours these are manufactured by my friend Malcolm Barlow.'

"Can I have a look?'

"It didn't take long for him take the top off and he said, 'Wow, wonderful. Can I meet him.'

"He's very worried about you.'

"The best thing he's done is copied mine perfectly where others have tried with alterations that aren't as good."

The Australians trained together on the Solent after sailing the boats from Dunkirk to Cowes and built confidence by filling major placings in club races over the inshore Admiral's Cup courses in the week before the series, which the British team did not contest. In one of them, the Around the Island race, Caprice tried out the new Brookes and Gatehouse electronic wind and performance instruments that were to become standard items on offshore racers.

"Major Gatehouse had built three sets of instruments for his first production run; gave the first two to British team yachts Quiver IV and Noryema IV and gave us the third. Graham Newland did a marvellous job fitting the instruments in three hours in time for the Around the Island race where Major Gatehouse had told us it would take at least two or three days and was confident we wouldn't be able to use it. Steering the boat by the instruments around The Nab at night, Graham said, Gordon, I can tell you exactly when the genoa is going to lift without looking at it.' And downwind they were excellent. Graham said, 'You can see the wind coming at the correct angle and set the sails up to get maximum speed. There is no doubt the Brookes & Gatehouse stuff really helped us. In a speech I made over there I thanked Major Gatehouse and the Brits got very upset about it. He only gave it to us because we didn't have the expertise to use it the new British boats had.'"

ON ARRIVAL IN England, the crew found the anti-fouling on Caprice's hull had been 'cooked' during the voyage and was flaking off. They slipped her and spent hours sanding it all off. "In many places it was down to the bare Huon pine – we didn't repaint it until after the series and we ended up with a very smooth bottom," Ingate said. "Maybe this is one of the reasons the boat did so well."

Bill Fesq, who had navigated small ships in British waters with the Royal Navy in World War Two, discovered that Southampton University had a full working model of the Solent currents for use by commercial shipping. "He went and spent probably a week studying it while we were scrubbing the boat down," said Ingate. "Every one of the crew had a vital

Unloading in England, Caprice shows her classic lines / INGATE FAMILY ARCHIVE

part to play in what became a fantastic effort but I put down Bill Fesq number one for his navigation, Graham Newland number two for the detail he put into the boat, then the rest of the crew and me. The Brits came up to us afterwards and said, 'You showed us how to sail in our home waters.'"

Besides Fesq's studies, to gain knowledge of England's spectacular south-west coastline, Ingate, Newland and Reynolds hired a car and visited every point of land between the Solent and the Lizard. "It was a great trip," said Ingate. "We did it in a brand new Mini Minor and we looked at every single point because if we wanted to get inshore out of the current we knew the places we would be looking at on the depth sounder and the charts. Bill, spending his time at the university, and our time looking down from the shore stood us in good stead. We had much more confidence and some very nice places to visit."

AUSTRALIA FINISHED SECOND in the Admiral's Cup to Great Britain, ahead of the Netherlands, USA, France, Sweden, Ireland and Germany. Although she had only just scraped into the team, Caprice was its star performer, winning the first three of the four races, to the surprise of everyone, including Ingate. The relatively smooth waters

Australian Admiral's Cup team, Cowes, 1965 / INGATE FAMILY ARCHIVE

suited her fine metre-yacht lines and Ingate, experienced in one-design racing and with an engineer's talent for getting the best performance from his yacht, was in his element in the rough and tumble of Cowes Week racing, dodging non-Admiral's Cup yachts, day-tripper launches, ferries and shoals amid swirling three-knot currents.

Caprice made a brilliant start to the Channel race, getting away from the rest of the fleet quickly under shy spinnaker, helped by a jockey pole broadening the angle of the brace, which Ingate favoured and was unused in Britain at the time, to gain a big break on the reach across the Channel to Le Havre. "Bill Fesq picked the Le Havre mark right on the nose," said Ingate, "Amazing considering the currents."

Caprice won, Camille was fourth and Freya eighth. The British team took the lead by four points from Australia with a second by Dennis Miller's new S&S43 Firebrand, third from Ron Amey's 45-footer Noreyma and sixth from the 46ft Quiver IV (Ron Clarke), a pair of new Camper and Nicholson designs.

Caprice won the second race, a 33-miler on the Solent for the Britannia Cup, after making a good start, in moderate winds of up to 20 knots that had her rolling downwind under spinnaker. At the end of the first

Caprice in the 1965 Admiral's Cup / BEKEN OF COWES

lap, Freya and Camille failed to pass through a gate set by the Royal Yacht Squadron off the Cowes Green to compact the fleet for the spectators. Freya, realising her mistake, returned to pass through it correctly to place 14th on corrected time after losing at least 20 minutes. Camille finished the race before her crew realised they had not read the sailing instructions correctly. They sailed the whole course again to pick up six points for the team. Britain with Noreyma IV second, Quiver IV third and Firebrand fifth, streaked ahead on the scoreboard with 195 points to Australia's 165.

Bill Fesq called a winning move for Caprice in the New York Yacht Club Cup, another Solent 30-miler, in strong winds that favoured the bigger yachts, which shot away in the early stages of the race. Caprice was well back starting the last windward beat, against the tide from a mark off Ryde. Fesq insisted that she head for Osborne Bay on the Isle of

Caprice crew at the Admiral's Cup, from left: Bill Fesq John Saalfeld, Gordon Reynolds, Gordon Ingate, Graham Newland, Fred Thomas, Mick York / INGATE FAMILY ARCHIVE

Wight shore while the rest of the fleet tacked off for shallow water with less current on the Southampton shore on the other side of The Solent. "Within five or ten minutes they disappeared out of sight, going into four knots of current," said Ingate. "'Don't tack, don't tack until I tell you to tack,' Bill insisted. We went around Ryde Middle in about 100th place and I said to Bill 'this not going to be our best race.'

"He said, 'Don't worry about it Gordon, we'll be alright.' Bill's down below – I could hear rattle, rattle, rattle – playing liar dice at the chart table. We went in until we were almost aground tacking up the island shore," said Ingate. "As we came into the windward mark the others, coming in from Southampton, were getting pushed down by the current and boat after boat was taking our stern. It was quite incredible. We went around the mark and the boat we were racing to the finishing line was Caper, an American 70-footer steered by Bus Mosbacher. It was unbelievable; we were the only boat that went that way and Bill said the tide suited him perfectly from what he had learned from the model."

Earlier in that race, Caprice had a brush with royalty. "Going up the Lymington shore we were racing boat for boat with Bloodhound with Prince Philip on the helm. He was trying to get an inside overlap on us. Fesqy was saying to me, 'Don't worry, Gordon, he draws about nine feet and we draw six foot four, keep going.' We all thought we were going to get a call for water and at one stage I can remember Prince Philip, being English and proper, saying, 'Oh excuse me, I would like to go about.'

"I said, 'that's not the right call.'

"At this stage, I am sure his keel was hitting the bottom because suddenly he went backwards and the overlap was broken. Gordon Reynolds, who thought there had been a call for water, let the genoa sheet go and I went absolutely haywire and said, 'You stupid, silly bastard, don't do that.' Bill Fesq hit me and said 'Don't you … look who's alongside' and right there Prince Charles and Princess Anne were right in the bow of Bloodhound, about ten feet away and heard every word. I thought, 'I'm in trouble.' So, when I got an invitation to go aboard the Royal yacht Britannia for a cocktail party that night, I thought I was going to be hauled over the coals but it was exactly the opposite. The Duke of Edinburgh congratulated me and said 'How could you in a 45-footer beat me in a 60-footer?' I said, 'you need to put on a bigger propeller.' Bill Fesq, standing right alongside me, gave me a big kick in the ankles. Someone had told Prince Philip by having a small propeller you reduce the drag but boy, did it make the handicap go up. A bigger propeller would have given them a more favourable handicap."

While Caprice won, Freya was ninth and Camille tenth. Britain suffered a setback with Firebrand disqualified for hitting a rounding mark. But a third and a sixth for Quiver IV and Noreyma IV meant that Britain went into the triple-scoring Fastnet race with a 14-point advantage over Australia.

The 605n miler, from the start at Cowes to the Fastnet Rock off the south-eastern corner of Ireland and return to finish at Plymouth, was sailed in following to beam winds rarely exceeding 20 knots. The Australian yachts were well placed at the Rock, with Caprice rounding ahead of her British rivals. But there, the British team gained its winning break by sailing east out into the Atlantic while the Australian yachts stood west into the Irish Sea, expecting a forecast wind shift. Instead, the wind moved back to the south-east, giving the British yachts a fast, free-sheet course for the leg back to the finish

Caprice rounding Fastnet Rock / CORK EXAMINER

in Plymouth. Quiver IV was first Admiral's Cupper with Noreyma IV third and Firebrand ninth. Camille placed fifth, Caprice seventh and Freya 11th.

Caprice's Fastnet Rock rounding was marked by an expensive incident. Captain John Illingworth, who had won the first Sydney-Hobart race in 1945 skippering Rani, was sailing in the Fastnet. He took Ingate aside one evening at a party beforehand and said: "Gordon, do you realise you have to pay a toll to go in the Fastnet race."

"'What do you mean John? I don't understand that.'

"'The only way you are going to get around the Fastnet Rock, you must pay a toll to Brian Boru, the king of the little people of Ireland. It must be an English shilling; he only accepts English money. Please go and get an English shilling and make sure you give it to him."

"So, we were rounding the island in the early hours of the morning and I stood up in the stern of the boat and shouted, 'Here's your toll King Brian' raised my arm and tossed the English shilling towards the Rock. At the same time, my Rolex watch flew off my wrist and followed it, still ticking away and I said, 'You bastard King Brian, you've not only got your English shilling, you've got my Rolex watch as well.'

Ingate steering with Fastnet Rock in the background and his Rolex watch overboard / INGATE FAMILY ARCHIVE

"IT WAS THE coldest race I can ever remember," said Ingate. "At the start I was again up the mast trying to put a crosstree back in its socket. It had become chewed away at the end. I cut four inches off the crosstree and stuck it back in the mast at the start. Thank heavens it was light. We just had enough thread on the turnbuckle to get the shroud tight. When we came back to Australia and the boat was going so well, I cut four inches off the other crosstree and stuck it back in.

"Caprice was the highest point scorer but the team sailed very well. Robert Clark, the designer, came aboard in England, looked at the boat and said, 'Wow'. Tears were streaming down his face and he said, 'What a beautiful boat.'"

Final points were: Britain 420, Australia 376, Netherlands 316, USA 313, France 231, Sweden 182, Ireland 163, Germany 53.

TEN YEARS LATER, after a reunion of Caprice's 1965 Admiral's Cup crew, Graham Newland, in a 'thank you' letter to Ingate, wrote: "I cannot tell you how much we enjoyed meeting the whole crew again and having a good yarn about the greatest yachting experience I ever had. You know you really started something in '65. I am quite sure that Caprice and the crew you put together heralded the beginning of modern ocean racing. Many of the techniques and practices that were evolved on Caprice are now standard practice all over the world. Even the rules have been changed to cope with the things that we started. You can be very proud of Caprice and the unbelievable record she established in 1965."

Between his other sailing commitments, Ingate continued racing Caprice with the Cruising Yacht Club of Australia fleet and making headlines for his mannerisms. If a crisis developed on the foredeck, he would impatiently dash forward to help solve it leaving the always-calm Mick Morris to take the helm. He also liked to wear formal yachting caps. A few miles off Bondi one Saturday, on the way back to Sydney in a Janzoon Trophy race, a loose sheet flicked his yachting cap overboard. Ingate dived straight over the side, retrieved the cap and trod water while his crew manoeuvred the 45-footer back to him. They had to make three passes before they got him back aboard and it cost them ten minutes but Caprice still finished third behind Taurus and Ragamuffin. "I treasure that cap. The commodore of the Royal Norwegian Yacht Club gave it to me when I won the Scandinavian Gold Cup in 1969," he said.

In the 1967 Sydney to Brisbane race, a crew mutiny saved Caprice from disaster. Bill Manning, the navigator, relates: "The fleet was about 20 yachts, the forecast a hard sou 'westerly all the way. Favourites to win line honours were the biggest yachts in the fleet, Caprice and Peter Hill's 40ft plastic fantastic Boomerang (a downhill flyer of fibreglass foam core sandwich construction).

"We set off from Sydney in about 20 knots of south-westerly as forecast. By the second evening, approaching the Solitary Islands, the wind and seaway had increased considerably to 30 knots, gusting to 40. Caprice and Boomerang were going neck and neck in a five-metre swell.

Fred Thomas (left) and Gordon Ingate with the trophies Caprice won at the 1965 Admiral's Cup

1972 Sydney-Hobart race, Caprice approaching the finish / BOB ROSS

Caprice's rig was full main with a boom preventer led to the bow and vang to the leeward rail and a storm spinnaker with a double kicker, again forward to the bow. We had the spinnaker sheet hard down on the leeward rail at the shrouds to narrow the spinnaker's opening to the wind and reduce the rolling of the boat.

"The steering was handled by one man sitting to windward pulling the tiller and a second man sitting to leeward with his feet on the tiller. When the boat started to luff in the puffs the man to windward would shout 'push'. The leeward tiller pusher would extend his legs, pushing the tiller to its maximum and disappear under the water now filling the cockpit. Caprice was on starboard tack, averaging about 10 knots and reaching 15 knots going down the waves.

"At about 2000 hrs it

American Eagle finishing the 1972 Hobart race / BOB ROSS

was quite dark and we spotted a stern light crossing our bow by no more than 100 metres. It was Boomerang on port gybe heading inshore to avoid the south-setting current. (Experienced sailors will quite rightly question the strength of the set on the third day of a southerly and big sea.)

"Gordon then shouts, 'Prepare to gybe' to the amazement of the crew who are not at all looking forward to the gybe. 'There are bricks in there,' we told Gordon. His reply was, 'We go in on port until we hear the surf and then gybe out again.' The crew mutinied and Gordon went to bed sulking, muttering as he went that we had lost him the race and wasted all the money that he had spent preparing for it. He stayed in his bunk and missed the remaining night watches.

"At sun-up, we looked for Boomerang, but although she had been only 100 metres ahead during the night, she was nowhere to be seen at 0650. We were very quiet and downhearted, assuming Gordon was correct about the set. To break the silence, we turned on the ABC news: 'Here is the seven o'clock news, there is a yacht aground on South Solitary Island.' Cheers from the crew got Gordon out of his bunk. We went on to win the race on handicap as well as taking line honours.

"Peter Hill and Peter Kurts, who was navigating Boomerang, told us later that Boomerang was following the Gordon Ingate method of navigating; listening for the surf in the dark. However, they were in the surf when they attempted to gybe out from the shore; not on South Solitary Island but the mainland of Australia some ten miles to the west. When they ran ashore with all sails set there was pandemonium on board with Peter Kurts sending out Mayday calls and the crew attempting to take

Race fleet in Constitution Dock after the 1972 Hobart race finish / BOB ROSS

the sails down. This all stopped when the forward hand came aft and advised they could jump off the boat without getting their feet wet. Aerial photos showed Boomerang had grounded at Fifty Metre beach between two rocks. She was towed off with substantial damage two days later. Gordon did thank us for refusing to gybe onto port."

Caprice years onwards in immaculate condition under the ownership of David Champtaloup / BOB ROSS

GORDON'S LAST SYDNEY-HOBART race with Caprice was in 1972 when, he says, he was denied the win by a measurer's error. Ted Turner's converted Twelve Metre American Eagle took line honours and won on corrected time as well after slowing seriously in calms on Storm Bay and in the Derwent River. Caprice had a chance of winning next day but was also slowed by calms and variable winds, finally finishing 26min 53sec too late.

Ingate claims Caprice was the real winner. "I was perfectly happy to come second but one day at the end of January Gordon Marshall (Chief Measurer NSW) rang me and said: 'Gordon, you've come first in the Hobart race. We calculated the age allowance on American Eagle incorrectly and you beat her by 21 minutes.'

"What are you going to do about that?

"'We can't do anything and it's too late to protest.'

"And I said, 'If I continue to go ocean racing I will raise a protest flag at the start. If you are not going to do anything about it, I will not race with the CYCA again,' which I didn't."

INGATE ALSO REMEMBERS the 1962 Hobart race for the after-race shenanigans at Constitution Dock initiated by Rupert Murdoch's lieutenant in his media business, Curley Brydon, who crewed aboard young Murdoch's 59ft John Alden design ketch Ilina and his crew-mate Don Mickleborough. Although every other race yacht in the dock had thrown a party Huey Long, the American owner of the line honours

Delphine with Don Mickleborough
INGATE ARCHIVE

winner Ondine, as sparse with funds as he was flush with dollars, had not.

Rupert and Curly decided Ondine should have a party anyway. Long was away in Launceston, trying to round up evidence for a protest so Mickleborough had a relation up there send a telegram in Long's name to Sven Joffs, Ondine's paid skipper, to make the boat ready for a party. They had embossed invitations printed: 'You are invited to a small informal party aboard Ondine, drinks 8pm' and delivered hundreds of them: Waterside workers, hospital staff – all were invited with wives.

The conspirators then organised 18-gallon kegs of beer and set them up around the dock with the word that Ondine herself was out of bounds. The party was a great success. The Lord Mayor turned up and apparently enjoyed himself.

Huey Long, however, was furious. When he heard about the party, he tried to charter a plane to leave Tasmania.

Brydon and Mickleborough, again aboard Ilina, famously initiated mischief in Hobart after the 1964 Sydney-Hobart race in which Ilina had a memorable duel at the head of the fleet with Peter Warner's 73ft schooner Astor.

They were both becalmed, dead level, off Maria Island 84n miles from the finish. Astor got going first to take line honours by 2hr 18min from Ilina.

The keen rivalry continued in Hobart. Brydon and Mickleborough, concerned at crew-mate George Pearce's inability to find female companionship, were smitten by a plan as they viewed a striking mannequin in the window display of Delphine's frock shop.

They went in, bought an eye-damaged version of the same model for 40 pounds, outfitted her with sunglasses, to hide the injury, a wig and smart dress and presented her to Raw Meat.

The model Delphine quickly became a Constitution Dock celebrity; so much so that Astor's crew one night kidnapped her and took her on a brief cruise down the d'Entrecasteaux Channel to Dover.

Ilina's crew drove to Dover, recaptured Delphine along with a naval ensign and hats from the naval cadets in Astor's crew.

A capitulation was arranged. Ilina returned the naval ensign and hats to Astor. Astor then returned Delphine to Ilina.

Ilina's crew, however, could not resist an opportunity to further complicate the proceedings. For the prizegiving at Hobart's City Hall, they dressed Dottie Sawyer, a lady friend of Curly Brydon, in the Delphine wig, sunglasses and dress and carried her in rigid form onto the stage.

Before a line-up of dignitaries including the Governor of Tasmania an infuriated Merv Davey, secretary of the Cruising Yacht Club of Australia, hissed: 'Get this thing off here and poked Delphine/Dottie in the boobs.

Dottie sat upright and said: "Get your hands off me!"

Davey fell backwards in shock. The CYCA banned all Ilina crew members from the club for six months and Ilina and/or her crew from racing to Hobart until suitable apologies were made to the Tasmanian dignitaries.

"During the suspension, we used to buy beer from the Bayswater Hotel and carry it down to Southerly (moored on the CYCA marina) for a drink," said Mickleborough. "We would get 30 or more people down there, more than at the club bar. At the end of three months, the club gave us a welcome back party."

7

OLYMPICS IN TEMPEST CLASS

INGATE, IN 1969, DECIDED TO return to the Olympic classes and seek selection in the Australian team for the 1972 Games at Kiel, Germany. He had sailed a season in Stars in 1958, tried Solings without being impressed, then decided to campaign in the Tempest, a new class where he could start at the same level as everybody else.

"The 5.5s were out of the Olympics, I didn't think I had a chance in the Dragons, I'll have a go at the Solings," Ingate said. But after a couple of sails in the Solings at Royal Prince Alfred Yacht Club, with the skipper as well as the two crew members having to hang out in the hiking straps, he found sailing the Soling was very hard work. "I went back to the Alfreds one night after racing and said, 'this is too hard for me.'"

Gerry Garrett, the former Australian Bluebird champion suggested: "Gordon, why don't have a go at the Tempest? The crew is on trapeze and if the skipper hangs out you are overloaded."

"I went for a sail, it was really easy," said Ingate.

Ingate and Rob Thornton training on Sydney Harbour aboard Sou'wester / JOHN HEARDER

The Tempest, a one design two-man high performance 22ft keelboat, designed by Ian Proctor, convincingly won the 1965 trials to select a new Olympic keelboat. After racing in the 1972 and 1976 Games it was dropped from the Olympics. It is still raced with fleets in Germany, France, Switzerland, Austria, United Kingdom and North America. In Australia, after reaching a peak of 15 boats, it declined with the loss of Olympic status and no longer races as a class.

Unusually for a keelboat, the Tempest also has a trapeze, so it is just as exciting to sail as a fast dinghy but is much more forgiving and cannot capsize. Due to the planing hull shape and large sail plan, the Tempest is remarkably fast when sailing on a reach, and achieves

Controls complexity on Ian Spies' Solemnity
JOHN HEARDER

Traminer (Jim Hardy/Max Whitnall) on Sydney Harbour, 1962 / BOB ROSS

speeds of more than 15 knots in moderate winds.

Ingate ordered a new Tempest from German builder Mader in 1971, along with Australians Jim Hardy, Craig Whitworth, Jim Dempster and Ian Spies and meantime bought the Australian champion Sou'wester from Bruce Jeffery.

It was one of the first six Tempests built in Australia by Geoff Baker's Fibreglass Yachts in 1967-68. "The boat would have been five or six years old, it was very soft," said Ingate. He started racing with youngster Michael Green as crew, but soon found he needed more crew weight and tried different crew members until he was joined by Rob Thornton, a hefty member of the Gretel and Dame Pattie America's Cup crews, who was living in Melbourne, became available for the Olympic trials there.

INGATE, WHO HAD never won a race in the class, immediately clicked with Thornton, winning three of the seven heats in the national championship, conducted by Royal Melbourne Yacht Squadron before the Olympic trials to finish in an unbreakable tie for first place with defending champion Gerry Garrett, crewed by David Champtaloup, in Contango II, Ingate discarding a fifth and Garrett a fourth. Established class leaders Craig Whitworth (former Flying Dutchman national champion), Gretel II skipper and former world 505 champion Jim Hardy, John Parrington, another former world 505 champion and Ian Spies, a former Heron and NS14 star, were never in the running. Ingate had a new set of sails by Hugh Treharne and was fast in the moderate sou'-wester conditions on Port Phillip. "We don't start to really fire until the breeze gets up to the 10 to 20 knot range and then she goes like a blur," Ingate said at the time.

In the Olympic trials Sou'wester shot away to four successive wins and finished the series with a third and two seconds for a loss of only six points, 18.7 points ahead of Ingate's nearest rival, Craig Whitworth, steering Man's Best Friend. "Bobby Thornton was incredible," said Ingate. "He was the right weight for the boat."

GAMESMANSHIP MAY HAVE helped.

Man's Best Friend (Craig Whitworth), Sydney Harbour 1962 / BOB ROSS

Before the trials Ingate questioned the practice of sand-blasting the interiors of certain Tempest hulls and adding reinforcing ribs and stringers to stiffen them, a practice that had been followed overseas, which had led to Jim Hardy changing hulls. "I don't think Jim Hardy has forgiven me to this day. Jim's argument was it wasn't cheating but keeping up with the Europeans."

A fortnight before leaving for Melbourne, Ingate stopped racing and spent a lot of time preparing the boat. He and Thornton fine-sanded the bottom and the keel, made a new rudder because the old one was slightly bent and made a new boom. He and Thornton set up the rig to especially suit the Port Phillip sea breeze.

In an interview with Peter Campbell of Modern Boating, Ingate said: "We found, with the sea breeze that one tack was entirely different to the other. Many people set their boats up equally on both sides but

1972 Olympic trials Melbourne. Sou'wester (Gordon Ingate/ Rob Thornton}, 1972 Olympic trials Melbourne / BOB ROSS

we found it much better to set the boat up unequally. On one tack you would have all the speed you wanted but you couldn't point because the waves would prevent it. On the other tack you would need to go as high as possible because the shape of the wave demanded that you take it absolutely head-on. So we set the boat up quite differently on port and starboard tacks, particularly the jib sheet setting and shroud tension. This paid off, as the moment we went on port tack I'd say the boat was invincible. The speed and pointing ability on port tack was probably our main winning margin."

While the Australian Yachting Federation, after the selection trials in March said, in a letter dated March 25, to the Australian Olympic Federation that Ingate and Thornton were among the six crews to be approved to compete in the Olympic regatta Kiel, commencing on August 21, the AYF did not receive official confirmation from the AOF that Ingate and Thornton were in the team until June 29.

Inclusion of the Tempest had increased the number of classes in the Olympics from five to six. The Australian Olympic Federation had not budgeted for a sixth class in its preliminary planning and had stated that only 13 yachtsmen (11 sailors and two reserves) could go to the Games. So, the AOF made Ingate/Thornton's selection in the full team of 16 (14 sailors, two reserves), subject to a 'satisfactory performance' on a European campaign in May.

On April 6, after a last-minute rush and some uncertainty as to whether space could be found, Sou'wester was loaded aboard the container ship Botany Bay in Melbourne. Ingate and Thornton flew to Europe courtesy of Qantas early in May where they picked up the boat at Zeebrugge in Belgium and trailed it to France for the European championship beginning on May 11. After that they drove 1,000 miles to race at Kiel Week, then returned to Australia for a spell before the Olympics in August. "The trip was made possible by the policy of the Australian Tempest Association to send the Australian champion crew to the world championship each year to gain international experience," said Ingate. "As there is no world championship this year, we chose the next biggest regatta, the European championship."

Ingate and Thornton finished ninth in a fleet of 40 in the European championship at La Rochelle, better than they had expected. They had to retire from the first race with a broken diamond stay and then scored 9-7-9-11-13 placings. They beat a former world champion Cliff Norbury of Britain into tenth place. Among other top competitors they headed was Pedre Lund of Norway, silver medallist in the Star class at the 1968 Olympics.

Contango (Gerry Garrett/David Champteloup), 1972
Olympic trials, Melbourne / BOB ROSS

The result was pleasing considering the quality of the opposition and the lack of preparation time Ingate and Thornton had before the championship. They had to ship Sou'wester to Europe after the Olympic trials in Melbourne without attending to necessary maintenance and improvements.

"Our boat is the oldest and looks the worst prepared related to the sophisticated expensive gear mostly supplied by the country," Ingate said afterwards. "All entries were allowed three mains, three jibs, three spinnakers, two masts, two booms, etc etc. We have one main, one jib and two spinnakers. All things considered I think we did bloody well and all teams, except Australia, receive government financial help."

They finished 19th out of 37 starters at Kiel Week (June 3-10), the best of all the Australian crews, on the Olympic Games course. "Kiel Week was a series of light fickle winds with major shifts," Ingate recorded at the time. "Maximum wind all week was half an hour at 12 knots; average 5-6 knots. The last race was abandoned through lack of wind; local knowledge was essential."

After Kiel Week, Ingate and Thornton returned to Australia for a spell before the Games, which began on August 29. Back in Australia Ingate, without success, sought to replace Sou'wester's hull, either by a new hull built in Australia by the registered builder (Fibreglass Yachts), chartering an existing approved hull in Australia, or purchasing or chartering an approved hull in Europe.

In the letter dated July 3 to the Australian Yachting Federation secretary John Shaw, he wrote: "I have already established contact with the owner of Tempest No G62, which was built by Dubdam Ltd of Holland and holds a valid German certificate. The owner would be interested in negotiating a deal with me. The problem arises of acceptance of this hull by the International Yacht Racing Union as additional stiffening, in the form of ribs and stringers, has been added contrary to the latest official class plans and specifications. Also, it would appear that the thickness of the hull varies between the bow and the stern making the boat stiffer in the forward region. These variances to the specification were also noted in other boats, particularly K78, H2 and S7, all having valid (national?) certificates.

"We ask the AYF to approach the IYRU measurer for clarification on these points as it is probably the lack of stiffeners that has caused the hull of Sou'wester to deteriorate and with it, lose performance."

If the arrangement to build or charter a boat in Australia was approved, Ingate asked that the AYF through the AOF arrange air freight free of charge, if possible. He added: "Most top-line competitors at the Kiel regatta who have spent some years in the Tempest class advised me of this problem of the Tempest hull 'going soft' and have had their hulls replaced. If we are to be truly competitive at the 1972 Olympic Games we ask the AYF for every assistance."

A setback was having the number one mast bent during shipping from Australia. In Kiel, the Australian Flying Dutchman skipper Mark Bethwaite offered to straighten it by inserting it in the fork of a tree and leaning on it – an accepted practice in dinghies at the time. Instead, the mast broke. "So we had to use the old mast and the old boat," said Ingate. "That's the sort of thing that made the whole Olympics a complete nightmare."

Rob Thornton (left) and Gordon Ingate, packed up for the 1972 Olympics / INGATE ARCHIVE

INGATE AND THORNTON were completely outclassed in the Olympics, finishing third last in a fleet of 21. "We were the oldest, longest, heaviest crew at the Olympics so we were pushing it uphill to start with," he said. Ingate regrets not being allowed to go ahead with a new boat for the Games as David Forbes had in the Star class and Bob Miller had in Solings and blames Craig Whitworth. "He basically said to the Australian Yachting Federation, 'Ingate has won in Sou'wester; if he takes any other boat he should take my boat', which was a brand-new boat called Man's Best Friend. I said, 'What about Dave Forbes, who won the Star class in an older boat and then went off and bought the best Star boat you could buy?'"

David Forbes, crewed by John Anderson, sailing Simba V won the gold medal in the Stars; John Cuneo, Tom Anderson and John Shaw sailing Wyuna won the gold medal in the Dragon class, for Australia's best medal haul at the Olympics to that date.

After the Games, Ingate expressed his feelings in a report to team manager David Linacre: "In asking for a report on my participation as a member of the world's top ranking 1972 Olympic yachting team, places added stress on the fact that I feel so badly about my results that I never cease to be amazed that we do rank as number one when the team is forced to carry a 19th in the Tempest class.

"David, I had a miserable time at the Games and I am trying desperately to forget them. I have nobody but myself to blame for allowing such a state of affairs to occur in the first place. I was and still am in a fantastic state of depression for which I am now seeking medical advice. I would like to apologise to you and the other team members for my behaviour. Being 'sent to Coventry' by my own volition was no fun to say the least.

"Because of the above maybe some good can come of it in this respect. The Australian Olympic Federation sends two doctors to look after the team and I think a great deal of thought should be put into the psychological aspects of the mental stress on Olympic team members. A psychiatrist or psychologist could be of far greater assistance than is at present considered. Other countries more knowledgeable than Australia in this respect do have such professionals in attendance. I understand from conversation that other sections and members of the Australian team were similarly affected; particularly the rowing squad and our number one swimmer. There is a tremendous amount in the subject I have raised, namely mental stress and its effects, which have a great deal to do with the final results. Note: our two (sailing) medallists had been before and were not overawed by the responsibility. They were both conscious of the problem of mental stress and knowledgeable enough to avoid or at least cope with it.

"I cannot emphasise strongly enough the fundamental mistake of the Australian Olympic Federation in not immediately supporting the Australian Yachting Federation's nominations. To be finally nominated on July 12 (the selection trials were held in March) was nigh on criminal. I would hate to think that any individual would have to be subjected to such an ordeal again. Both Bob and I, when finally told of the decision, had the same reaction – 'tell them to get stuffed'. This reaction of course was gradually becoming evident as far back as May after competing at La Rochelle.

"The AYF must share some criticism in nominating their team in priority order. I do not think they should announce the nominations other than alphabetically and their International Yacht Racing Union representative should be fired.

"To be expected to arrange one's affairs, family and business, financial etc in such a short time, let alone give thought and action as regards the boat, all added to the strain, conflict and confusion.

"I realise in retrospect that because of the mental and physical state I found myself in at the time of departure that I should not have gone at all. All it did was to add weight to the stupid premise of the AOF that they were vindicated in their original assessment not to send the Tempest class.

"In the March trials Sou'Wester was as good, if not better, than the subsequent three medallists in our class. That statement is made in all honesty. We were going so slowly and badly at Kiel that any one of the ten Australian competitors would have beaten us.

"The AYF must be congratulated in all aspects of sending their team ahead. To the federation members, officers and officials – particularly John Shaw (AYF secretary) – I tender my very best THANKS. I know the costs were high but the overall results certainly justified the outlay.

"I would like to add that the whole German organisation of the Olympic yachting was unbelievably superb and I will be surprised if is ever surpassed by any nation in the future.

"When it comes to consider the logistics of the Olympics, the Australian team organisation in general was excellent. Maybe some of the organisers are old, but obviously their experience is evident. But I still wonder where all the money goes.

"I have no complaints whatsoever about the food, clothing and lodging; all deserve top marks. In conclusion David I would say that your liberal, quiet but firm approach to your job as manager that you played no small part in Australia's success at Kiel."

Another regretful episode on the 1972 Olympic campaign befell Ingate while he had joined the Americans at a training camp they had set up beforehand at the Association Island camping ground on Lake Ontario where he met Hoyle Schweitzer, co-founder with Jim Drake, of the Windsurfer class. "I was sitting on the beach with some Tempest guys," said Ingate. "Up comes this young bloke, a German who can speak some English who said, 'I came here because I heard some of you might be interested in my new boat.' It was a board with a rope attached

Mast goes in wild conditions, 1965 CORK pre-Olympic regatta, Canada / BOB ROSS

to the boom to haul the sail out of the water. A couple of the young blokes tried it and wobbled off. It was the very first showing of the Windsurfer.

"I got on and my reaction was the same as Glenn's: 'Sorry son, this will never take off.' My brother-in-law, Bruce Symonds, had been offered the Windsurfer agency in Australia. When I came home I told him this story and said, 'It will never go anywhere' and to this day, he has never forgiven me."

Ingate continued racing in the Tempest class with Sou'-wester after the 1972 Olympics and won the Australian championship in 1973 and 1974. Crewed by Graham Ewing on Sou'-wester he won the Tempest class at the 1974 Dunhill Olympic classes regatta on Lake Macquarie. Overshadowed in the earlier races by Peter Hollis, the world Contender champion from Queensland sailing Solemnity, previously owned by Ian Spies, Ingate gradually got on top as the series went on. He was very fast upwind in the medium-light winds with new Elvstrøm sails.

Hollis won the first two races in strong winds, lost heat four to Ingate on a port/starboard protest and still scored three wins to Ingate's three. But the disqualification meant he had to carry a fifth in his final points tally while Ingate's discard was a third. The final points were: Sou'-wester (Gordon Ingate, NSW), 2-3-1-2-1-2-1, 9; Contango (Gerry Garrett, NSW), 4-2-3-1-2-3-2, 20.4; 3, Solemnity (Peter Hollis, Qld), 1-1-5-dsq-3-1-3, 21.4; 4, Tempo (Patrick McGregor, NSW), 6-7-2-3-6-5-4, 50.1; 5, Jippi II (B.Foley, NSW), 3-4-7-5-4-6-5, 53.4.

IN 1975, AT the second Dunhill Olympic classes regatta at Geelong, sailing Jippi II and crewed by Bill Solomons, Ingate finished second to Ian Spies skippering Gerry Garrett's Contango, with Garrett as crew. The upset of the regatta was all but sprung by Danish-born Jörn Hellner, formerly crew for the great Dragon sailor Eric Strain. Hellner, after going home for a time, had returned to Australia with a brand new Mader Tempest he called The Sting amongst his unaccompanied baggage.

John Cuneo was to have skippered the boat but after some preliminary tuning skirmishes on Corio Bay concluded they were not going well enough to have a chance and departed home to Queensland. Hellner skippered the boat himself with Sydney Flying Dutchman Olympian crew Tim Alexander finding himself transported from a nice holiday in Geelong to the trapeze wire. They won the first race, were disqualified from the second on the protest of Ingate for a mark-rounding brush, then scored 3-1-2 to take a clear eight points lead. As lack of experience in the class began to tell, they crumbled in the last two heats with fourth and fifth placings. Final points and placings: 1, Contango (I.Spies, NSW), 2-2-5-2-4-1-2, 20; 2, Jippi II (G.Ingate, NSW), 3-4-1-dsq-3-2-1, 22.4; 3, The Sting, (J.Hellner, NSW), 1-dsq-3-1-2-4-5, 26.7. 4,(P.MacGregor, NSW), 4-1-2-3-5-5-3,

Tempests can capsize but they don't sink; 1965 CORK regatta / BOB ROSS

Jippi II dismasted, Sydney Harbour; Ingate has a swig and Bill Solomons has a laugh / BOB ROSS

KA2 Sou-wester (Peter Hollis/Tom Anderson) clears out from a start, 1976 Olympic trials / BOB ROSS

32.4; 5, Sou'-Wester (W.Manning, NSW), 7-3-4-4-1-3-6, 39.1.

Four Tempests were in the Australian contingent for the CORK Pre-Olympic regatta at Kingston, Ontario, Canada in July 1975. Spies and Hellner sailed new Maders; Ingate and Patrick McGregor chartered boats. Spies finished 11th, Hellner 18th and Ingate 26th (4-25-22-dnf-28-dnf-22). Ingate, crewed by Graham Ewing, crossed in sixth place in race one then picked up two placings when two boats ahead of him were disqualified; one of them the Italian Giampero Dotti who, under spinnaker tried to sail through to windward of Ingate who, under jib, luffed. The jury upheld Ingate's protest that the Italian failed to respond.

HELLNER AND JAMES Byrne subsequently won 1976 Olympic team selection at the 1976 Dunhill Olympic Regatta on Port Phillip Bay, Mel-

KA6 Jippi II (Gordon Ingate/Bill Mobbs) in a handy windward position, 1976 Olympic trials / BOB ROSS

Contango (Gerry Garrett/Graeme Ewing) winning a race at the 1976 Olympic trials / BOB ROSS

bourne, by just 0.7 of a point from Queenslanders Peter Hollis and Tom Anderson sailing Sou'wester. In the last heat, with all others out of the running, Hellner/Byrne had to beat Hollis/Anderson and finish third or better as well to take the series.

Hollis sat on Hellner from the start and rounding the last mark they were fifth and sixth. The breeze freshened slightly, standing the chop up a little higher and Hellner's Mader found a little more speed. Hellner stood to the left to escape Hollis' cover and sailed into a header that gave him the opportunity to tack and cross two more boats to take the third pacing he needed.

Final points and placings for the leaders were: The Sting (J.Hellner, NSW), 2-3-4-2-1-dsq-1, 19.7; 2, Sou'wester (P.Hollis, Qld), 1-4-2-3-2-3-2, 20.4; 3, Contango (G.Garrett, NSW), 5-2-6-1-3-2-3, 27.4; 4, Marie (I.Spies, NSW), 4-1-1-4-4-4-5, 32. Ingate, crewed by Bill Mobbs, finished outside the top placings in the fleet of ten boats.

HELLNER, WELL REGARDED as a Dragon and Soling crew was having only his second season in Tempests. His major problem had been his inability to hold regular crew. He teamed with Byrne, a Melbourne Flying Dutchman sailor, just before the trials. They finished 10th out of 16 crews in the Games on Lake Ontario. Australian coach Mike Fletcher said they had suffered through lack of a training partner in their pre-Olympic campaigning overseas. They did improve in the second half of the regatta, which was won by John Albrechtson (Sweden) with 4-1-2-1-7-2-1-10 placings. Hellner/Byrne's placings were 14-13-10-14-4-8-9.

The Tempest never gained the wide international support expected for an Olympic class and was dropped from the schedule for the Moscow Games in 1980. The British Tempest crew Alan Warren and David Hunt, former world and European champions and the silver medallist at Kiel in 1972, in disgust after finishing 14th overall in the 1976 Games, doused their six-year-old boat Gift Horse with acetone and set fire to it on the tow in, stepped off onto a support boat and recited a Viking funeral oration as 'The Orse', as it had become known, sank into Lake Ontario.

8

AMERICA'S CUP CAMPAIGN 1966-67

SIR FRANK PACKER, ENCOURAGED BY the promising showing of his Twelve Metre Gretel in the 1962 America's Cup in which she won a race – the first challenger to do so since 1934 – before going down to the American defender Weatherly 1-4, challenged again for the Cup's 1967 edition. In the meantime, in September 1964, the British challenger Sovereign lost in four straight races to the American defender Constellation.

The Sydney newspaper proprietor was known to be a big 'punter' (one who bets on horses) and he had personally gambled £100,000 on Alan Payne being able to design a Twelve Metre yacht that could be competitive with the Americans, who had held the America's Cup, the world's major match-racing event, through 17 challenges since its inception in 1851.

Frank Packer, who was knighted in 1959 for his services to journalism, was a gravel-voiced, burly 6ft 2in former New South Wales amateur heavyweight boxing champion who built on the foundations of his father Robert Clyde Packer the Consolidated Press organisation, which published a daily and Sunday newspapers, a glossy women's magazine, financial weekly and had a controlling interest in the Channel 9 television station. He ruled that empire with a hands-on discipline, frugality and, sometimes irrational, sackings often with reinstatements the next day. Once in the lift he became annoyed at a lad who had caused it to shoot past his floor. Taking him to be one of his copy boys Sir Frank growled, "How much do you earn a week?" "Thirty shillings," the boy replied. "Take it and get out," said Sir Frank, digging the money out of his pocket. Later he discovered that the boy was a post office messenger. But he was fair, rewarded loyalty and helped many of his staffers in financial trouble with gifts and loans. He once bawled out a copy boy for being slovenly dressed, then gave him the money to buy a new suit.

The America's Cup became a talking point around the Australian yacht clubs when it became revived in 1958 using Twelve Metre class yachts and the US defender Columbia easily beat the British challenger Sceptre. Sir Frank was considering getting back into sailing. He had owned, from 1930 until 1942, the beautiful Fife-designed 65-footer Morna, which became scratch boat in the Royal Sydney Yacht Squadron fleet and he was thinking of building a 55-footer. Over a convivial lunch with Squadron friends Bill Northam and Richard Dickson, the suggestion was made that he build a Twelve Metre and challenge for the America's Cup. When an American reporter later asked him, what had led him into the America's Cup, Sir Frank replied: "Alcohol and delusions of grandeur."

Sir Frank and his advisers Northam and Dickson with Keith Martin, one of his executives at Consolidated Press, retained young Alan Payne, already well known for his ocean racer designs and secured the American Twelve Vim for crew training and as a yardstick for their new boat. They chartered Vim for four years from her owner John Mathews and shipped her to Australia for about $90,000. She was old, built in 1939 to a design by Olin Stephens, but fast. The 1958 defender Columbia, skippered by Briggs Cunningham, only narrowly won the defender trials from Vim, sailed by Bus Mosbacher.

After Payne had tested five-foot models of his design at the Stevens Institute at Hoboken, New Jersey and given assurances that he had a design faster than Vim, the syndicate was expanded to raise the $500,000 needed to build the challenger and ship her to Newport. The

Sir Frank Packer, surrounded by well-wishers and autograph hunters after Gretel's race win in the 1962 America's Cup / WARREN CLARKE, QANTAS

other major contributors were the Ampol Petroleum Company Limited and W.D. and H.O. Wills, the cigarette manufacturer.

Sir Frank said at the time: "We have probably got more chances at the first attempt of losing rather than winning. But as long as we put up a good show and it is not a walkover, the whole thing would have been worthwhile." One of his oldest employees said: "I've had my ups and down with the big fellow and hated him at times but I'm still a Packer man. I'd give anything to see him pull this yacht race off."

Gretel, skippered by Melbourne Olympian Jock Sturrock, did put on a good show against the US defender. Weatherly, designed by Phil Rhodes, skippered by Emil ('Bus') Mosbacher, won the first race by 3min 46secs in a 10-18 knot breeze. Gretel made history by winning race two, sailed over a 24n mile triangular course in an 18-25 knot breeze. Surfing under spinnaker, she passed Weatherly on the reaching leg to the finish to win by 47 seconds. Weatherly won race three by 8min 40sec in a light 8-10 knot breeze over a windward-return course. Race four over the triangular course was a close one in a six-knot breeze, with Weatherly winning by a mere 26sec. Weatherly won the deciding race five, over a windward-leeward course by 3min 40sec.

Gretel's crew hiking hard in the 1962 America's Cup / WARREN CLARKE, QANTAS

THE AUSTRALIANS WENT home believing they could win the America's Cup. The New York Yacht Club seemed to share that view. Within six weeks, shaken by Gretel's showing, the New York Yacht Club tightened loopholes in the Cup's deed of gift. No future challengers would be permitted to use American sails and sailcloth. The club also decreed that other equipment and services, including tank-testing of hull model facilities, could not be used unless they were absolutely unobtainable in the challenger's home country or elsewhere.

Sir Frank was keen to challenge again but had to wait until after the US defender, the Olin Stephens-designed Constellation skippered by Bob Bavier, cleaned out the British challenger Sovereign (Peter Scott) in four-straight races in 1958 by the whopping margins of 5min 34sec, 20min 24sec, 6min 33sec and 15min 40sec. Realising that the New York Yacht Club's new restrictions would apply only to new boats and could not be made retrospective, Sir Frank challenged again with Gretel. Cunningly, he said that Gretel would be 'repaired' below the waterline where in fact, Alan Payne was to completely redesign the underbody. All the sails and equipment acquired from the United States for the 1962 challenge could be retained.

Then, however, another Australian challenge emerged, initiated by Royal Melbourne Yacht Squadron Commodore Otto Meik, with Gretel's 1962 skipper Jock Sturrock, whose home city was Melbourne, as skipper. The designer was Warwick Hood, who had been working for Alan Payne and started his own design business after Payne had become unwell with hepatitis in 1963.

Commodore Meik pulled out after three or four months but a syndicate of Melbourne businessmen, headed by Emile Christensen, put together a strong, fully-sponsored, challenger contender, Dame Pattie. She was built by Billy Barnett at his Berry's Bay boatshed on Sydney Harbour through 1965 and 1966 while Halvorsen, Morson and Gowland, with Trevor Gowland the foreman shipwright, made the alterations to Gretel in another boatshed nearby on Berrys Bay.

Royal Sydney Yacht Squadron, the Challenger of Record club as it as it had been in 1962, was to conduct selection trials on the open waters off the Sydney coastline in early 1967. Meantime, crew training began aboard Vim, under crews skippered by Eric Strain, an Australian Dragon class champion (1958-59) and Gordon Ingate.

Ingate recalls a very typical Packer encounter at their first meeting in Sir Frank's Consolidated Press office when Sir Frank invited him to join his America's Cup campaign. Sir Frank was looking through the expenses claims from the reporting staff at a small side desk. "Sir Frank looks up from the petty cash dockets, sorting them into the ones he was going to pay and the ones he was going to query. He turns around and his first words were, 'Where's your hat?'

"I said, 'I don't wear a hat Sir Frank.'

"He said, 'Go out and buy one now.'

Vim's crew in early campaigning, from left: Bill Ridding, Peter Kershaw, Bill Manning, Mike Phiffer, Laurie Mardell, Gordon Ingate, Doug Patterson, Dennis Pilkington, Andy Thane, Bill Holyer, Rob Ogilvie, Bill Fesq / AUSTRALIAN CONSOLIDATED PRESS

"He gets up from a little desk and gets behind an enormous desk, the biggest desk I have ever seen and said, 'Okay Ingate, come and sit here. Congratulations on your effort at the Admiral's Cup.'

"Yes, Sir Frank, we did very well. I had a very good crew and the team generally made a few mistakes and didn't come out winners but for our first effort against the Brits we did well.'

"And he said, 'Would you like to join our America's Cup program?'

"I said, 'Yes, that sounds like another interesting program I would like to start on.'

"Have you ever sailed a Twelve Metre?"

"No.

"And he reached over to a big drawer inside this huge desk, pulled out a set of keys and said, 'These are the keys to Vim. Go and learn to sail it.'

"I thought 'Wow' and that was the beginning of the best period of sailing in my life. I didn't know what I was letting myself in for except Vim became basically my boat. I was responsible for it. I had to get my own crew; I had to negotiate with Trevor Gowland who was responsible for looking after the boat and Joe Pearce who was responsible for the sails. Vim was on a mooring in Neutral Bay, very close to where Joe Pearce had his sail loft. The first time I went on board, on my own, I opened it

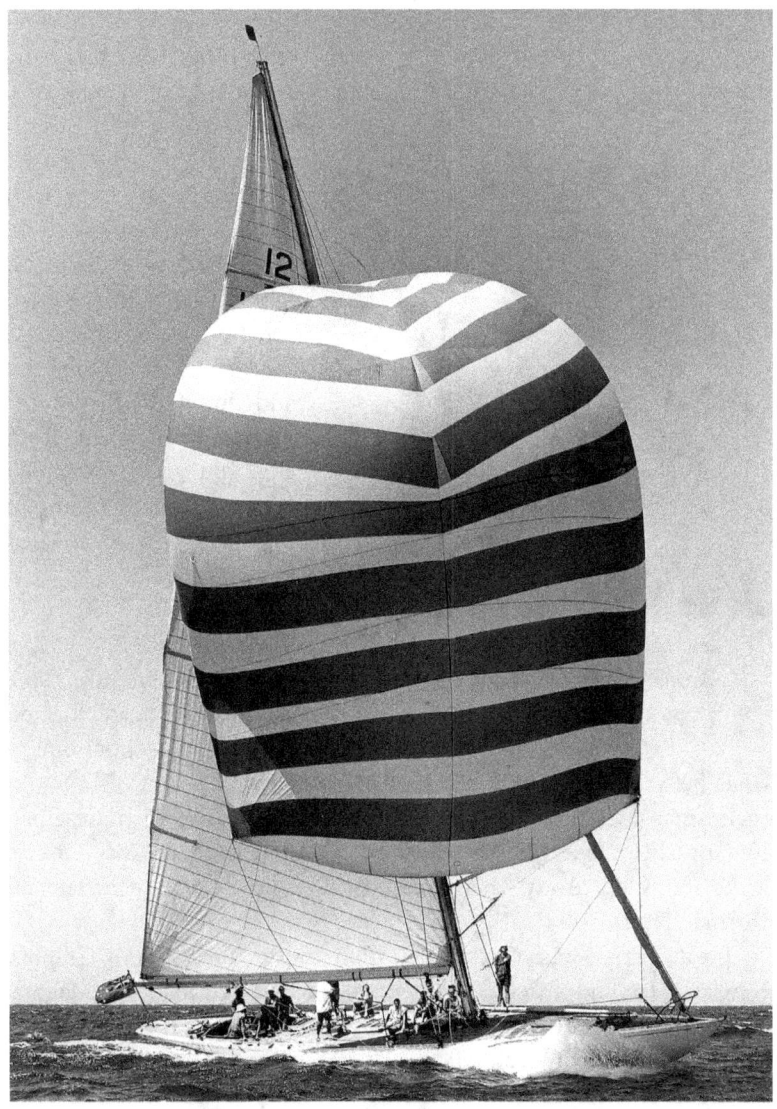

Vim under spinnaker/ DOUGLASS BAGLIN

up and went over the boat from bow to stern; looking into every nook and cranny. I spent the day on board and started to think about crew. I made a list of names and we managed to go for a sail, not with the full crew by any means; there might have been five or six of us on board. We learned how to haul up the sails with no-one there to tell us what

Key characters, from left: Colin Ryrie, Archie Robertson, Graham Newland
RYRIE FAMILY ARCHIVE

to do. It was really starting from scratch. We had a guy we called 'Lurch' on board, an employee of Consolidated Press who might have come out sailing with us the first time so he could report back to Sir Frank on how we handled the boat. We didn't do any mischief, we were able to come back and put it on the mooring without mishap. With a 30-ton yacht you don't get too much room to manoeuvre in a crowded mooring area."

AFTER GRETEL WAS re-launched in July 1966, Strain and Ingate formed crews for preliminary trials between Gretel and Vim. Strain's crew was: Cockpit: Eric Strain (helmsman), Colin Ryrie (tactician), Norman Longworth (navigator), Ken Beashel, Mike Moore. Midships: Trevor Gowland, Ross Grieve, Mike Ramsden, Andy Thane. Foredeck: Colin Betts, Mike Fletcher, Norman Hyett.

Ingate's crew was: Cockpit: Gordon Ingate (helmsman), Graham Newland (sailing master), Bill Fesq (tactician-navigator), Magnus Halvorsen. Midships: Bruce Anderson, Frank McNulty, Brian Northam, Doug Patterson. Foredeck: Mick York, Barry Russell, Bruce Stannard.

Ingate invited Jim (now 'Sir James') Hardy to join his crew after Hardy, crewed by Max Whitnall, won the 505 world championship in 1956, beating the fabled Dane Paul Elvstrøm into second place. Hardy went on to skipper Australian America's Cup challengers in 1970, 1974 and 1980. "I was responsible for getting Jim into the America's Cup scene," said Ingate. "We got on very well together; all the crew were prepared to learn and they did learn."

Eric Strain quit in the early stages of the program, in October 1966, at one of the regular Tuesday evening meetings of the key players Sir Frank held in the Consolidated Press building. Ingate recalls: "We were sitting down just talking about Twelve Metres and Eric Strain piped up, 'You can't expect us to do any good against Dame Pattie using these tired old sails'.

"Sir Frank said, 'I am using them because it gives us a leg over the Americans because we are allowed to use American sails in this challenge'.

"And Eric said, 'All I can say is you are a bloody fool.'

Eric Strain / RYRIE FAMILY ARCHIVE

"Sir Frank looked at him, 'Thank you for your comment Mister Strain, here's the door, leave and I never want to see you again.'

"Anyone else want to follow him?"

"Magnus Halvorsen stood up and followed him, as did others. I was standing there but kept my mouth shut, which is unusual for me. I am not going to criticise Sir Frank ever because gave me that opportunity to get into Twelve Metre racing. He was supplying the lunches, the drinks, waterproof gear and put in £100,000 of his cash before Noel Foley (W.D. and H.O. Wills) and Bill Walkley (Ampol) came along."

Dame Pattie was launched in August 1966 and officially christened in honour of the wife of Prime Minister Sir Robert Menzies. She trained alone each weekend over the next few months while Gretel and Vim continued racing.

In January 1967 Gretel and Dame Pattie held a series of 'working up' trials on an America's Cup course off Sydney Heads. Gretel's crew was: Helmsman Archie Robertson, who had been trial horse helmsman in the 1962 challenge, Bruce Anderson, Jim Hardy, Trevor Gowland, Norm Hyett, Peter Kershaw, Graham Newland, Frank McNulty, Barry Russell, Colin Ryrie, Paul Salmon and Mick York. Dame Pattie won the first race, in a moderate breeze, by 1min 35sec then walloped Gretel 8min 40sec in the second trial in a light breeze.

Trygve Halvorsen replaced Robertson at the helm for race three, sailed in a moderate breeze. Dame Pattie would have won by four minutes or more when she broke her mast 250 yards from the finish handing Gretel her only win in the series. The dismasting meant a delay of at least three trial days. Meantime Sir Frank and his advisers made their bold decision to alter Gretel and the Royal Sydney Yacht Squadron agreed to postpone the preliminary trials from February 25 to March 25.

In those first three races Gretel, always noted for her reaching speed, was still faster on this point of sailing but, on the Olympic course, which places more premium on windward performance, this had not been sufficient to allow her to catch Dame Pattie, which used all Australian-cloth working sails made by Joe Pearce, Pearce spinnakers and once or twice a very light Hood reaching spinnaker. Gretel used a Hood mainsail from 1962 in the first two trials and a Pearce mainsail from Hood cloth in the third trial. Neither sail looked as good as Dame Pattie's main although Gretel's main looked better in the third trial on her new oval-section bendy boom.

A frantic seven-week program, by an expert team of shipwrights headed by shipwright and Gretel crewman Trevor Gowland, re-shaped Gretel's hull, mainly making her forward sections finer to overcome her tendency to hobbyhorse in a seaway. The re-build also flared her after sections so that the genoa leads were about 9in out from their previous position on the gunwale to broaden the sheeting angle.

Dame Pattie, better organised, better sailed and faster upwind, continued her superiority in the preliminary trials, beating Gretel 6-1. During those trials Vim, skippered by Ingate, had shadowed them both on the first weekend of racing and appeared to be faster. "Although the sails were old, we learned how to get the best out of them and it dawned on me that this was a fast light-weather boat, she was just superb; a beautiful boat to sail." said Ingate. Initially Sir Frank gave permission for Vim to sail out to the course with Gretel and Dame Pattie and pace them at a distance around the race course. "We found we were holding them in our conditions, anything under 14 knots," said Ingate. "I went back to Sir Frank and told him we were doing pretty well against the other two boats. He said, 'Do you think you can beat them?'

"I said, 'given our conditions, yes.' 'Alright', he said, 'get closer and give them a go.' And we went out and beat both of them. We weren't allowed to start with them, or sail the same course and admittedly they were racing one another but when we parted company we were doing alright. Our spinnaker handling was better, we were doing well with the manoeuvres they were doing."

After Dame Pattie won the first three races, by margins of 2min 22sec, 4min 59sec and 5min 22sec, Sir Frank replaced Trygve Halvorsen with Ingate for race four in dramatic circumstances:

"I answered the 'phone about 7.30 in the morning of my birthday, a Wednesday.

"'Gordon Ingate, Frank here.'

"'I want you to sail Gretel today.'

"'It's a working day, I have to work for a boss.'

"'Ask him for time off.'

"The chairman of my company said, 'No, I want you in the office at nine o'clock.' I was the managing director of the company.

"I said, 'This is a very rare occasion for me, to sail in the America's Cup.'

"I arrived down at the wharf and the first bloke to come along was Trevor Gowland. I had been sailing Vim and we beat both of them the previous Saturday; Dame Pattie and Gretel. Vim was a bloody good boat.

"Trevor said, 'What are you doing here?'

"'Frank has asked me to sail the boat today'.

"Tryg Halvorsen had been sailing Gretel and lost all of the races against Dame Pattie."

"'Fuck,' he said and turned around and walked off.

"Colin Ryrie comes down, he was the tactician on the boat and said, 'What are you doing here Gordon?'

"'Sir Frank has asked me to sail the boat today' and he says, 'Fuck, over my dead body,' so he stalks off.

"About an hour later, they all come trooping down led by Colin Ryrie and they step on board the boat, not a word said. So, we come back in; Colin has not said a word to me the whole day. He must have been fired by Packer because we never saw him again."

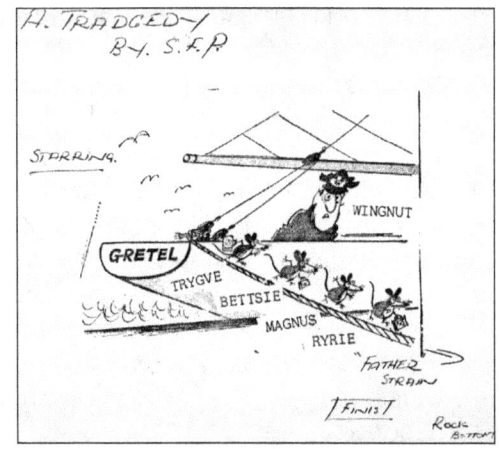

Cartoonist's view of Ingate's progression into Gretel / INGATE FAMILY ARCHIVE

DAME PATTIE WON race four in a light north-east breeze by 3min 6sec to go 4-0 up in the series but had to 'fight harder than in any of the other races so far', read a report in Packer's Daily Telegraph by his Channel 9 news director Mike Ramsden.

The next day, Ingate found he had been fired from his job as general manager of the aluminium fabrication firm Lightweight Structures, because he had disobeyed the chairman's direction to work instead of sailing Gretel. "Next day when I went into the office, my desk was cleared, nothing on it but a note that said, 'See me when you come in, leave the car keys on your desk'. I went to the boss's office, he said 'Right, we've decided that we don't need your services any longer, please leave the office.'

"I was a bit upset because I had built the business up mainly through my associates from sailing; engineers, architects; 90 percent of the work I got from the company came from my association with sailing.

"I walked out through the basement about a quarter past nine thinking, 'Hell's bells, that was a bit quick.' There was a telephone box opposite; at least I could let Sir Frank know I had been hit hard. Fairy (Sir Frank's secretary Kathleen Maisie Faircloth) answers the 'phone. 'Yes Gordon, what do you want? You had a good day yesterday.'

"I would like to come in and see Sir Frank and tell him about my situation.'

"I'm sure he'd love to see you, come in."

Ingate went into Consolidated Press and told Sir Frank: "I have just been fired because I sailed Gretel yesterday. It was a work day and my chairman insisted I go into work. I decided it was more important to my career to sail Gretel."

"Sir Frank, said, 'We'll see if we can fix that, Gordon, what can you tell me about the company?'

"I told him I had built the company up, was a 25 per cent shareholder and the chairman was a 75 per cent shareholder.

"He said, 'That's a boo boo on your part.' I told him I didn't have the money at the time and had spoken to the chairman about increasing my shareholding but the answer was always 'no'.

"'Right, let's see how we can do something about this. What's your bank?'

"'Commonwealth Bank of Australia.'

"'I know someone there. What's your overdraft?'

"'$100,000.'

"'Fairy, get me Charles on the 'phone.

"'Charles, I've got a chap here who knows a lot about one of your companies called Lightweight Structures and he's giving me some pretty bad news at the moment and I thought I had better pass it on to you so you can have a look at the company because he thought it might go downhill. Because his overdraft can go up to $100,000 I would like to get half of that overdraft. I thought you should know the company could be in trouble.' Sir Frank put the 'phone down and said, 'Gordon, the seed has been sewn.'

"'Where does he get his material from?'

"'The Australian Aluminium Company out at Auburn.'

"'He said 'I think I know the managing director out there. Fairy, get me so and so.'

"'I've got some information for you. You are dealing with a company called Lightweight Structures and the message is out they are likely to have some trouble. Be a bit tighter on supplying their material.'

"Sir Frank then said to me 'You say you've been fired and got nothing in writing? Right, what you need is a good lawyer, I am going to give you my lawyer.' He rang his lawyer and said, 'Fred, I am sending Gordon Ingate into you; he's got a problem and I want you to fix it.' I

Close battle on the second reach of race six in the preliminary trials
SYDNEY MORNING HERALD

First tack second beat, race six / SYDNEY MORNING HERALD

went and saw Fred and he managed to get the most in settlement out of Lightweight Structures because he just threatened to take them to the cleaners. Lightweight Structures were broke by Christmas; they crossed Sir Frank Packer."

Ingate, with sheet metal workers turned engineers Sam Rigby and Johnny Jones, then started the metal processing company Rigby Jones Pty Ltd. "Johnny became the foreman, Sam was the manager and I was just the investor. Sam was a very good Rugby player with Eastern Suburbs and got us a lot of business for his involvement in football as I had for Lightweight Structures through my connections in sailing."

Meanwhile, back on the race course, Dame Pattie won race five by 4min 48sec; Gretel won race six by 1min 9sec after Dame Pattie blew out three genoas in a 25-30 knot southerly. Gretel also had dramas with two crew members washed overboard, a broken backstay and sailing under mainsail alone after a sea burst her genoa 300 metres from the finish.

"It was horrifying; a tough, tough day," said Ingate. "The southerly was over 30 knots and, in those boats 30 knots is just trying to stay afloat, they are so big and heavy they just plough through the waves and water is coming in over the deck."

Ken Beashel, who was on board for the first time, was washed off the foredeck but managed to hang onto a dropped headsail and regained the

Gretel crew hunkered down / RYRIE FAMILY ARCHIVE

deck. Then Barry Russell, went overboard, hit by a sea as he was working on a damaged spinnaker pole, but managed to regain the deck 20ft from where he went in.

The backstay broke as Gretel rounded the first leeward mark of the triangular-windward-return course. She sailed the next two windward-return legs without the backstay. "We realised we would lose the mast if we didn't do something about it. Ken Beashel climbed inside the hull, tied bowline knots in the broken ends of the wire to link the backstay back together; a great feat in a big seaway."

RAINBOWS & DRAGONS

Gretel on the second beat of race six, 'a really tough day' / SYDNEY MORNING HERALD

PACKER'S TELEVISION STATION Channel Nine transmitted direct coverage of the racing. "The coverage was huge because Sir Frank wanted to watch the trials. The general manager of Nine said, 'But Sir Frank, that is going to cost us an awful lot of money because we should be showing the shows we get income from.'

"Sir Frank said, 'If you don't like it I will take my tower away'; he owned the station's transmitting tower at Willoughby.

"Bill Northam was doing the commentary. Filling in time he said, 'I am doing quite well as a businessman and the company I work for, (Johnson and Johnson); we don't make the best product in the world, but we are next to it (he was referring to tampons)'. That went over live on Channel 9."

The final three trial races were held on May 5, 6 and 7 in extremely light east-northeast winds of 3 to 10 knots and smooth seas. Dame Pattie won the first by 3min 12sec, after Gretel was in the lead twice on a 24n miles course off Sydney Heads. Dame Pattie won the remaining two races; the second by 9min 31 sec and the last by a whopping 24min 11sec.

Dame Pattie's genoa begins to tear
SYDNEY MORNING HERALD

Gretel's crew was: Afterguard: Gordon Ingate (helmsman), Graham Newland (navigator/tactician), Jim Hardy. For'ard hands: Mick Young, Barry Russell, Paul Salmon. Waist and winchmen: Frank McNulty, Trevor Gowland, Norm Hyett, Ken Beashel. Dame Pattie's crew was: Jock Sturrock (helmsman), Norm Wright (navigator), Bill Barnett, Norm Booth. For'ard hands: Pod O'Donnell, John Taylor, Ed Beacham. Waist and winchmen: Bob Thornton, Richard Dickson, Doc Greenaway, John Freedman.

Gretel approaches the finish under mainsail alone to win by 1min 2sec
AUSTRALIAN CONSOLIDATED PRESS

GRETEL'S TRIAL CAMPAIGN had been hampered by bad helmsman choices, crew dissension, resignations and/or sackings. And there was the possibility that a final alteration by designer Alan Payne, which shortened sail area to the extent that Gretel had to sail with a 10-man instead the usual 11-man crew under the Twelve Metre rule, made her slower in the under 10 knot winds that prevailed in all three races. Overall Dame Pattie won 11 of the total 13 trial races and lost the other two through gear failures.

Two days after the last race Sir Frank announced that his syndicate had decided not to send Gretel to Newport for final trials against Dame Pattie, as he had originally intended.

He sportingly offered Gretel and all her equipment to the Dame Pattie syndicate if they wished to use her as a trial horse. They did take some of the sails and other spare gear, but elected to hire the American Twelve Nefertiti as trial horse in Newport.

First of the three races in the final trials series; close in light air
SYDNEY MORNING HERALD

Ingate had tried to persuade Sir Frank to let him take Gretel to Newport, for final trials against Dame Pattie. "Winning in Sydney has got nothing to do with the boat's capability; it has to be done in Newport", he told Sir Frank. "That means making the boat lighter and having a much bigger mainsail. I will try and get a syndicate together to take the boat over to Newport. He said, 'You can do what you like Gordon, but I am not going to support you in any way, but you've got my permission to take the boat.'

"I made a few enquiries and the response was good but the money wasn't coming quickly enough. Dame Pattie was already on the ship."

The America's Cup match between Dame Pattie and the new Stephens design Intrepid, skippered by Bus Mosbacher was an anticlimax with Intrepid, an average two percent faster over the 24.3n-mile course. Intrepid won the first race by 5min 58sec in 18-knot breeze; the second by 3min 36sec in a seven-knot breeze which suited Dame Pattie. Dame Pattie was no match for Intrepid in the fresher 12-16 knot of race three with Intrepid's winning margin 4min 41sec. And Intrepid won the fourth race, in the 10 to 12 knot breeze for which Dame Pattie had been expressly designed, by 3min 35ec, gaining more than a minute on each windward beat.

Sir Frank Packer, who had watched most of the races with Alan Payne, quickly lodged another challenge through the Royal Sydney Yacht Squadron for 1970. He engaged Alan Payne full time to draw him a new boat, supervise its building and crew training. Payne had the experience and quiet but authoritative presence to command the respect of Sir Frank and the crewmen. There were to be no more mutinies.

Start of finals race two
AUSTRALIAN CONSOLIDATED PRESS

Beaten but unbowed, Gretel crew after losing race three of the finals
AUSTRALIAN CONSOLIDATED PRESS

9

GRETEL II AMERICA'S CUP CHALLENGE

GORDON INGATE RE-ENTERED THE TWELVE Metre arena in June 1976 when he organised a syndicate of Sydney businessmen to purchase Gretel II from Alan Bond, who had used the innovative Alan Payne design as a training and tuning boat for his failed 1974 America's Cup challenge with Southern Cross. Skippered by Jim Hardy, she had been a strong challenger for Sir Frank Packer in the 1970 America's Cup; winning a race, losing another after crossing the finishing line first on a controversial protest before going down 1-4 to the US defender Intrepid. The scoreboard didn't indicate how good a boat Gretel II was. There was a general belief among the experienced observers at Newport that Gretel II was a faster boat than Intrepid but the crew had lacked hard racing. There had been no opposing syndicate in Australia that year. By the time the America's Cup series began, Intrepid's crew had sailed 33 match races to survive the US defender trials. Gretel II had sailed just four to beat the French challenge candidate France.

In June 1976 Ingate and his close friend Bill Manning, who had been navigator on Ingate's successful offshore racer Caprice of Huon, formed a syndicate of businessmen/yachtsmen to challenge for the 1977 America's Cup through the Royal Sydney Yacht Squadron and buy Gretel II from Alan Bond whose challenge was then in doubt after he failed to negotiate a fresh deal with designers Bob Miller and Johan Valentijn after his 1974 challenger Southern Cross was thrashed. Jim Hardy's attempt to form a challenge for the RSYS through the Matilda syndicate had also folded. The organising committee for Ingate's challenge was Bill Northam (chairman), Sir William Pettingell, Richard Dickson, Peter Holmes a'Court, Ingate, A.W. Byrne, J.B. Reid and Norman B. Rydge Jr. Bill Manning was executive officer and manager of the association.

Ingate, who had been looking for a new boat to replace his ageing ocean racer Caprice of Huon, considered buying Gretel II and converting her into an ocean racer, as Jock Sturrock had done with Gretel. If Hardy's challenge did not materialise, he could take the opportunity to become the RSYS challenger for the America's Cup. He had made a study of the 1974 series, comparing the finishing times between Intrepid and Courageous and Southern Cross and practice sessions between Gretel and Southern Cross and concluded that Gretel II would have been as good as Courageous in some conditions.

He first approached Alan Bond about buying Gretel II in December 1975 but the price nominated by Bond was too high. Bill Manning recalls: "It was at a party at Mick York's waterfront home at Drummoyne for skippers and crews entered in the Sydney-Hobart race and Bondy was there along with other yachting notables. Gordon and myself discussed the purchase of G2 with Bondy and we made good progress broadly involving the price and what would be included. We began planning the syndicate composition and getting the boat to Sydney. All was going well with the syndicate agreeing to the price and syndicate member John Reid's contacts, as a director of BHP, involving sea transport to Sydney. We recruited Norm Hyett to go to Yanchep with Gordon to take possession of the boat and gear and get it on a BHP heavy-lift ship from Fremantle to Sydney. In June 1976 Bond, whose challenge was still in doubt, called Ingate who made an offer that Bond accepted."

Ingate recalled: "Bondy said he wanted $90,000 in cash on delivery of the boat and they (the organising committee) said 'Under no circumstances are you going to give Alan Bond money for the boat because he doesn't own anything.' Sir William had been dealing with him in Santos

Walking the plank at Gretel II's Berrys Bay berth, 1976 / BOB ROSS

– they were both on the board – and said, 'He is an absolute crook; you are not to deal with him personally.' They found that the boat was owned by a two-dollar company owned by Bond Corporation Holdings, a public company. Bond had 52 proprietary companies with a paid-up capital of two dollars." So Ingate's organising committee drew a bank cheque for $90,000 made out to one of those companies, Southern Cross Properties Pty Ltd. "I was to make the deal with Bond. Dick Dickson, the chairman of Brambles at the time, organised the transport; to pick up the boat at Yanchep Sun City, transport it on a Brambles truck down to Fremantle to be put on a BHP heavy-lift ship that was carrying coal to and from Newcastle."

In the handover at Yanchep, the residential township and boat harbour north of Perth that Bond had developed, Bond first gave Ingate notes prepared by John Cuneo, who had skippered Gretel II in the warn-up trials against Southern Cross. "The notes contained everything you needed to know about campaigning a Twelve Metre," said Ingate. "Cuneo was very meticulous in recording the preparations. The truck driver comes around and interrupts while we are talking; 'Excuse me sir, are you happy for me to take the boat?'

"'Yes.'

"'Please sign here' in the truckies' book.'

"He gives Alan a copy on a small piece of paper. I am talking to Alan a bit away from the truck and the boat. The driver gets into the truck, starts the engine and takes off with a huge roar, smoke and dust. Alan's nickname was 'Toad' from Wind in the Willows. When he gets excited he jumps up and down."

New aluminium deck sealed openings / BOB ROSS

"'Where's he going, where's he going? I haven't got the money yet.'

"'Don't worry Alan, here's the money.'

"I gave him the envelope. He ripped it open and said, 'You bastard Ingate'. It was a bank cheque for $90,000 made out to Southern Cross Properties Pty Ltd, so Bondy, who was looking forward to pocketing the cheque into his personal account, couldn't touch it; he would get into trouble if he laundered it and he knew that. If I had given him cash I would never have got the title to that boat. He wasn't a very nice bloke to do business with. He never spoke to me for six years. He never owned anything; his house, all those paintings."

Bill Manning adds: "All was going so well that it emboldened Gordon to think we could do anything. He phoned me from Fremantle and told me to contact Brambles and get a tug and a barge to meet the ship off Sydney Heads where he would organise for G2

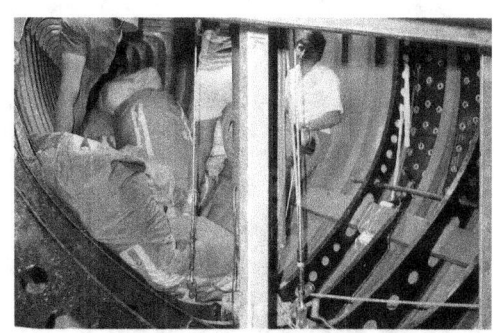

Aluminium stiffening structure around the mast
BOB ROSS

Graham Newland and Bruce Gould / BOB ROSS

to be loaded onto the barge with its own loading gear. It was winter and the sea would be calm said Gordon; then move the barge and G2 plus all the gear to Halvorsen's boatshed at Ryde. I said to Gordon that this was an ambitious arrangement that would not work. In the end we determined the boat should go to Halvorsen, Morson and Gowland's boatshed at Ryde. Trevor Gowland did a marvellous job organising the transport by road from Newcastle to Wyong, even though it stopped traffic and blacked out the electric lights in Wyong for most of the day and later to Sydney."

ALAN PAYNE RE-DESIGNED Gretel II with the aim of improving her proven capabilities in light to moderate winds, gambling a little on these conditions being experienced at Newport, Rhode Island and to best handle the spectator chop. He made the hull much finer forward

Light day training / INGATE FAMILY ARCHIVE

Smile for the camera, Gretel II training on Sydney Harbour 1977 / BOB ROSS

to let her go through the waves a little more easily and to get more sail area within the rule; shortened the measured length by taking out about 3,000 lb of ballast to let the hull float higher. Payne pushed the stern post forward and a bigger rudder was fitted to make Gretel II easier to steer. The keel was made thinner and a new aluminium deck was fitted with the cockpits and hatches designed to meet the requirements of the change to the rule intended to do away with the big deck openings that were regarded as unseaworthy and to keep the crew above deck. "I had been doing a fair bit of racing with Glen Foster (the American Tempest sailor) at that stage who said the name of the game at Newport was the number of spectator boats that turned up, so you had to have a boat for light weather and this bloody chop," said Ingate. "That's what we did with Gretel II; she had the biggest sail area ever put on a Twelve Metre."

THE ALTERATIONS WERE made by Halvorsen, Morson and Gowland at Wyong with Oregon and Queensland maple again used in the hull rebuild. The alteration was due to be completed by the end of January, leaving little time to assemble and train crew before Gretel II was due to be shipped to Newport in May. That meant falling back on a core of America's Cup and offshore racing veterans. They called themselves 'Dad's Navy' and the tee-shirts the Gretel II crew wore in Newport told

Gretel II crew training offshore, 1977 / ROSS

the story: 'Daughters of America, lock up your mothers;' a subversion of the historical adage 'Mothers of America, lock up your daughters.'

The crew was: Gordon Ingate (skipper and helmsman), Graham Newland (tactician-navigator), Peter Cole (mainsheet), Rob Ogilvie (sheet tailer), Mark Ross (cockpit), Dick Lawson (sheet tailer), John Freedman (winch hand), Graham Brown (winchman), Bruce Gould (forward hand), Graham Ewing (forward hand), Jack Christoffersen (forward hand). Team manager: Bill Manning. Reserves: Joe Cooper, Leon Cremer, Bill Dewar, Geoff Gale, David Kellett, Gordon Marshall (navigator), Peter Nicholson. Tender driver: George Bate.

FOLLOWING A RECONCILIATION with designers Bob Miller (who changed his name to Ben Lexcen on February 27, 1977) and Johan Valentijn, Alan Bond entered a challenge through the Sun City Yacht Club, with a new Twelve called Australia, to be skippered by Noel Robins, the Australian champion in the Soling class keelboat. The Australian syndicates, east and west, prepared in isolation, later in Newport as well as

Newport, crew and support staff:- Front row, left to right: Graham Newland, Bill Dewar, Mark Ross, Jack Gale, George Bate, Graeme Brown, Bill Manning. Second row: Jack Christoffersen, Gordon Marshall, Peter Cole, Gordon Ingate, Dick Lawson, Graham Ewing. Back row: Leon Cremer, David Kellett, Geoff Gale, John Freedman, Joe Cooper, Peter Nicholson, Bob Ogilvy, Bruce Gould / INGATE FAMILY ARCHIVE

Australia; ultimately a telling factor against Australia in the America's Cup match.

IN NEWPORT, GRETEL II and Australia had to sail in a challenger elimination series, organised by the Yacht Club d'Hyères of France as Challenger of Record, against Sweden's new Sverige, designed and skippered by Pelle Petterson, Baron Bich's Andre Mauric design France and Australia. The challengers had plenty of racing, firstly in a round robin series from August 4 to August 9 in which each yacht raced each of the other yachts three times with one point awarded for each win. The results of the round robin decided the pairing of the semi-finals with the boat having the most wins meeting the boat with the least wins while the boats having won the second and third most races met each other. The

Newport locals welcome Australians, Old Colony house / PAUL DARLING

Gretel II weigh-in, Newport 1977
PAUL DARLING

semi-finals were decided by the best four out of seven races for each pair. The finals were decided by the best four out of seven races. The round robin win scores were: Australia 6, Gretel II 4, Sverige 4, France 0. Gretel II handed Australia her only defeat in the round-robin, by 4min 25sec in a six-knot light air breeze.

IN THE SEMI-FINALS, Sverige won the first race, sailed in a nine-knot breeze, by 2min 7sec; Gretel II won the second in a 9-12 knot breeze after gaining the lead on the run before the finish of triangle-windward-return-windward course. Gretel, which had lost the start to Sverige, almost caught her on the first beat then overlaid the windward mark to round 2min 43sec behind. Gretel gained seven seconds on the second reach, another 24sec on the second beat. She took the lead on the run to round 16sec ahead. Sverige initiated a tacking duel on the beat to the finish. Gretel II covered until Ingate, realising that Sverige was gaining, broke off the duel and concentrated on sailing fast to win by 58sec.

Sverige broke her mast on the second beat of race three, while smacking into a rough wave pattern raised by a 16-20 knot wind, after rounding the leeward mark 2min 30sec ahead, handing Gretel II the win. Sverige won race four, in a 12-knot wind, by 53sec and after a lay day, requested by Gretel II, race five by 2min 11sec from Gretel II in a 12-16 knot breeze. Gretel II won race six on August 20, in 12-15 knots, by 45sec after Sverige crossed the starting line early and had to restart. Gretel II won, despite having torn two genoas, to even the score at three-all.

Ingate concentrates / INGATE ARCHIVE

On the morning of the seventh race the following day (August 21), with racing scheduled to end on August 22 at end of racing that day, under the Conditions Governing Selection of Challenger, Ingate wanted to call a lay day, anticipating lighter breeze that would suit Gretel II on August 22, for which winds of under 15 knots had been forecast. And if there could be no more racing Gretel II would win by three races to two because in the event of a tie, the Conditions ruled that Sverige's win in the first race would be discounted. But Bill Fesq, who was Royal Sydney Yacht Squadron Commodore, as well as being a Gretel II team member, said, "No Gordon, we are not going to claim a lay day; that is not sportsmanship."

Gretel II leads France, challenger eliminations, Newport / INGATE ARCHIVE

"'We are entitled to it; I think I am allowed to, I am the skipper.'
"'If you do Gordon, I will withdraw our challenge on behalf of the RSYS.'
"Unbelievable," said Ingate.

Sverige won the start of deciding race seven after Gretel II lost seven seconds in a recall and led around all marks in a 10-13 knot breeze to win by 1min 58sec. Experienced America's Cup observer Ted Jones in his book Challenge '77 suggests that the selection of the wrong genoa at the start may have cost Gretel II the race and the series: "Opting for their three and a-half ounce genoa at the start, they found it too light for the wind they encountered on the first leg. When they came together, the light genoa did not provide Gretel II with the power to stay with Sverige and with its draft pulled aft, because of the stronger than optimum wind for that genoa, they were unable to point high enough to backwind the Swedes. Both Ingate (who served as tactician) and Graham Newland (who steered) admitted later that this was the turning point of the race. Both knew at that moment it was all over. Later during that first leg they changed to their six-ounce genoa, but it was too late."

INGATE WAS GRACIOUS in defeat. At the press conference after the last race, he congratulated Pelle Petterson: "He's obviously designed,

First meeting, Australia and Gretel II, Newport / PAUL DARLING

Traditional dumping of Gretel II's skipper after the last race / INGATE ARCHIVE

produced and organised a fabulous boat and I would like to pay my respects to the Swedish challenge. They've obviously put something together for the first time in very, very good order indeed. It was a good series, other than the last race; it's hard to be able to put exactly the reasons we lost but I think probably we were beaten by a better boat, a better skipper and a better organisation."

"In defeat, the Aussies were about as sorrowful as other crews would have been in victory," wrote Ted Jones in Challenge '77. "After passing Fort Wetherill, Gretel flew her spinnaker all the way into Newport Harbour. Their dock was edge-to-edge people. They were greeted by a rousing cheer. Champagne corks popped and virtually everyone in reach went for a swim. They are a happy bunch, good sportsmen, the underdogs, the darlings of the summer, but now they were out. But defeated? Never!"

Australia went on to beat Sverige 4-0 in the challenger final trials sailed in light to moderate breezes but went down to US defender Courageous, designed by Sparkman & Stephens and skippered by Ted Turner, 0-4 in the America's Cup match. Ingate believes Gretel II could have beaten Australia in the final. "We had beaten Australia around the America's Cup course by 13 minutes in light air. Australia races Courageous and the maximum breeze was 14 knots. Courageous just killed her four-nil." He also believes that Gretel II would have beaten Courageous because subsequently she did beat her in the Twelve Metre world championship, sailed in Fremantle in 1986 as a prelude to the 1987 America's Cup. "We just trounced Courageous," he said.

Although the Gretel II team lost, they had won popularity with the people of Newport. "While the sailing competition was tough, the social life was even tougher," recalled crewman Leon Cremer. The crew spent more than six weeks living at a former mansion called The White Elephant and enjoyed the vibrant Newport nightlife. Bill ('Bubbles') Manning, was in charge of team security, "a big problem," said Ingate. "He drove the crew bus, a converted laundry van we called 'Bubbles' Bus' and he used to go around town picking up the stragglers. Jack Christoffersen was the main problem; it seemed he could get by with practically no sleep. We'd go around The White Elephant, 'Is everybody in bed?'

"'Yes, goodnight Gordon,' while half the crew were down in the town. You could never find Jacko. We had one super party where we had the Newport jazz band, they were very popular and an old dinghy filled with ice and Australian booze and wine. We became very popular with the locals."

They made good contacts in the police force and the fire brigade. Bill Manning recalls: "The Swedes were staying at Hammersmith Farm. I organised a police escort for Bubbles' Bus and told them, 'When you turn into the drive I want some sirens and lights please.' This wall of red and blue lights and sirens coming up the drive scared some of the Swedes out of the place. We subsequently found out they thought it was a police raid."

Ingate bought Gretel II in 1978 and regularly sailed her in Sydney Harbour races through the summer of 1978-79 with hopes of returning to Newport as the Royal Sydney Yacht Squadron's challenger for the 1980 match. He sailed in just about every race open to her including social Wednesday afternoon and twilight races, at least proving that Twelve Metres can be campaigned like any other one-design keelboat without an engine or attendant motor launch. He still believed strongly that Gretel II was good enough for a third try at the Cup. "I believe the races between ourselves and Sverige and Australia showed that Gretel II is not a spent force," he said. "We were in striking distance and the only reason we did fail was the lack of experience of the skipper and the crew. I can trace everything to something the crew or myself did wrong."

However, in November 1978, the syndicate that had supported Gretel II in the 1977 challenge, decided that it could not raise the money to give Alan Payne a hope of designing a competitive boat in the time for the challenge it had entered for 1980. Ingate had asked the Squadron not to withdraw the challenge until the last possible moment, but he agreed that Gretel II should not be nominated until he and his crew had proven themselves so he decided to enter Gretel II in the new Twelve

Metre world championship, to be sailed from Brighton, UK, in September 1979.

Before Gretel II left for England she was altered again at Cockatoo Island, Sydney, with refinements of the changes Alan Payne had designed for the boat for 1977. The lead keel was fined down and its bottom given more vee. "The whole fin is a very gentle shape without bumps," said Payne. Much of the lead carved from the keel was transferred to the inside of the hull as internal ballast. There was a relatively small loss of displacement; about 200lb. A trim tab was new and had a slightly different shape. The big rudder Payne put on the boat for 1977, in place of the very small one which Jim Hardy and John Cuneo found difficult to steer with, was replaced by a smaller one with a much fairer shape. Special attention was given to fairing the junction between the rudder and the skeg. The most intriguing alteration was the small, flat transom Payne put on the bustle, reminiscent of US challenge contender Mariner's underwater square back of 1974. Instead of torturing the waterlines around to a measurement point, Payne had chopped them off square. "It's a minor thing really," said Payne. "It does achieve a degree of separation of flow."

Payne said the changes should lead to speed improvements. "They've made it a nicer boat, again intended for light weather. Her stability has been reduced still further and it was pretty miserable to start with, we are praying for light weather." Ingate said that although the newer aluminium Twelves did have more favourable weight distribution than the wooden boats like Gretel II, that was only an advantage in a chop. Weight in the ends did not matter so much in smooth water and all the recent testing had shown the criteria Payne used in re-designing Gretel II towards short waterline, minimum displacement and maximum sail area was the right way to go.

The Hood loft in Sydney flattened out the mainsail to extend its range into fresher winds. Ingate had stored all the sails used at Newport after the 1977 challenge and would use them in England. Graham Newland, his backup helmsman in Newport, re-joined him for England with the significant new title of co-helmsman and tactician, while John Keown, an experienced offshore navigator, was navigator. The only other crewmen from 1977 were Mark Ross and Graham Brown. The new crew members were Gordon's son Stephen, Peter Costello, Adrian Barwell, Mike Maxwell, Chris May and Bruce Edwards.

Ingate secured free shipping for Gretel II to Europe, picking up the offer made by US shipping magnate Henry Mercer, the owner of the

Match racing Australia off Fremantle, November 1979 / INGATE ARCHIVE

1962 US defender Weatherly, who in 1962 promised Sir Frank Packer to continue transporting Australian Twelves free of charge. While Gretel II was being unloaded in the port of Zeebrugge, Belgium, there was drama. "The ship takes off for Bremerhaven, we are trying to put the boat together to sail across to England and we discover the gooseneck is missing. We had last seen it laying on its own on the deck. We drove from Zeebrugge all through the night to Bremerhaven where the ship is anchored off. We chartered a boat to get us out there, went aboard the ship believing the gooseneck had probably gone overboard. I went on the deck where the boat had been and there was the gooseneck, sitting in the scuppers."

Gretel II crossed The Channel on a moonlight night under shy spinnaker, carefully, never attempting to cross a ship and arrived at Brighton where the tide was at its 18ft low. Ingate said to his crew: "There's the wharf fellows. How are we going to get up there?" The crew had to wait six hours for the tide to roar back into the marina.

Britain's new America's Cup challenger Lionheart, skippered by John Oakeley, won the world championship by two points from Sweden's Sverige (Pelle Petterson) eight, with Gretel II third on nine points. Fourth was the 1964 America's Cup winner Constellation, which had become Lionheart's pacemaker, skippered by Guy Gurney. Lionheart won the second fleet practice race, sailed in perfect conditions, by four minutes from Sverige with Constellation third and Gretel II, steered by Graham Newland, fourth. She went on to take the world championship, sailed on a match-racing basis, without once being headed across the finishing line. British sailing journalist Jack Knights wrote: "The sorry thing is that Gretel II is no longer an all-rounder she once undoubtedly was. Neither did the seasoned Newland enjoy much success behind her twin wheels. Some of his starts were wildly off."

SHIPPED BACK TO Fremantle, WA, Gretel II in November 1979 match-raced against Australia, being campaigned again for the 1980 America's Cup. Noel Robins skippered Australia with designer Ben Lexcen as tactician. The re-designed Australia comfortably beat Gretel II four-straight in the David Brand Memorial Trophy series with winning margins of 6min 55sec, 5min 42sec, 4min 42sec and 2min 20sec. Lexcen's re-designed hull featured a finer and deeper bustle that shifted the centre of buoyancy aft; a sharpening of the leading edge of the keel with profile added to the back of the trim tab, a deeper and finer rudder. The changes improved the boat's balance, enabled it to carry more powerful sails, sheeted more closely and made it easier to steer with less use of keel trim tab. Lexcen was enthusiastic about the performance figures Australia recorded during the series. "We are miles faster than we were in 1977," he said. "I think we have jumped a whole generation of boats if the numbers are right."

Although Australia won every race comfortably, Gretel II did show Australia to be vulnerable in light air, upwind and down. Gretel II, optimised for light air performance by designer Alan Payne, was no match for Australia once the wind freshened to 15 knots, not quite as fast in the 10-15 knot range, but faster in eight knots and under. Ingate did not sail as well as he can, perhaps trying to do too much. Graham Newland, his co-helmsman of 1977 and the world championship, was not available for the David Brand series. In his place, Ingate took Mick Morris as tactician while the experienced John Keown was navigator. Morris had sailed many sea miles with Ingate on Caprice of Huon and did a lot of the steering while Ingate concentrated on tuning, trim, tactics and crew management. Ingate did all the steering during the David Brand series, feeling that Morris had not had enough experience with the Twelves.

Alan Bond, through his challenge manager Warren Jones, recruited Jim Hardy to skipper Australia in three series of trial races against Gretel II off the Sydney coastline. With extra ballast added, Gretel II was at her fastest in the last series in March, winning two of the six races. But Australia had been deliberately slowed by allowing growth to gather on the hull. Australia won the first two races sailed over an America's Cup style course, shortened to 18n miles in an 8-10 knot breeze by 3min 38sec and 2min 1sec. Gretel II won the start of the second race but Australia powered through to the lead two-thirds of the way up the first beat after a hot tacking duel.

On the second day, Australia won the first race by 2min 40sec in light variable breeze; Gretel II, after winning the start, won the second by 25sec and on the third day, over very short courses, Gretel II won the first race by 20sec, after winning the start in a five-knot breeze while Australia won the second in freshening wind by 2min 30sec. Jim Hardy said the series was very useful. "For starters, I had not been steering a Twelve Metre for six years while Gordon Ingate seems to have been sailing Gretel II every day. I certainly needed the miles under my belt, particularly working up with Jack Baxter (navigator) and Ben Lexcen (tactician). By the end of the American summer I hope we will be, as Ben says, as close a combination as Newcombe and Roche (tennis greats)."

Australia made the 1980 America's Cup final after beating two tough competitors in the challenger elimination series. First, she squeaked through the semi-final against Sweden's Sverige 3-2 after breaking her mast in race two and then beat France 3 4-1.

Freedom, skippered by Dennis Conner, after an extremely thorough 15-month tuning and training program with Enterprise, a very similar Olin Stephens design, beat Australia 4-1 in the America's Cup match. Although Australia had beaten three other challengers, none of them offered the sort of competition Enterprise gave Freedom. Ben Lexcen took a late punt on adopting the broader mainsail set on a bendy top mast that had made the under-capitalised, poorly-managed, British challenger Lionheart immediately competitive in the early stages of the challenger elimination trials. Eventually, this rig gave Australia a speed advantage over Freedom in winds under 10 knots that enabled her to win a race, have a chance of winning another and gave her a 700-metre advantage in a third race, with one leg to go, when the time limit ran out.

WHILE SEEKING FUNDING for his 1977 America's Cup challenge with Gretel II, Ingate approached Kerry Packer, the son of Sir Frank Packer, who had become head of the Packer's Consolidated empire after the death of Sir Frank in 1974.

"I got Rupert Murdoch involved and tried to get Kerry Packer involved but Kerry hated the idea of the boats being called after his mother. He made it very clear He was not going to put any money into supporting my efforts with Gretel II because his father had called the boats Gretel, particularly with the second Gretel.

"He told me, 'I would be very happy if you took it out the Heads and sank it!'"

Ingate also clearly recalls his first meeting with Kerry Packer during the 1967 trials when he was steering Vim and Gretel against Dame Pattie.

"One night Frank and I were talking about his campaign in his office when there was a knock at the door.

"'Come in.'

"And Kerry walked in; he was about 18 or 19 and Frank said: 'Gordon, I want to introduce my idiot son to you.'

"I was taken aback.

"I don't think he realised Kerry was dyslectic but that made Kerry extremely clever with numbers. He was excellent at gambling and business."

10

GRETEL II, BENCHMARKER AUSTRALIA II 1983 AMERICA'S CUP

GORDON INGATE AFTER HIS TRIAL-HORSE role in Australia's 1980 America's Cup campaign continued to race Gretel II in everything going around Sydney Harbour and again generously campaigned her as a benchmark for Australia's three challengers with new boats for the Cup in 1983. First, he trialled against Syd Fischer's new unconventional Alan Payne design Advance and then sent Gretel II to Melbourne to race against the Bond syndicate's radical new Ben Lexcen wing-keeled design Australia II and the similar but more conventional Lexcen designed Victorian yacht Challenge 12 for the Advance Australia Cup in March.

Advance was launched on October 7, but its preparation was delayed while Fischer's syndicate continued to seek sponsorships and supporters in the depth of a depression. Although Fischer recruited the talented young 18ft skiff sailor Iain Murray – winner of six consecutive Giltinan international championships – as skipper, the syndicate found putting

Gretel II leads Advance in a tuning session on Sydney Harbour, December 1982 / BOB ROSS

a crew together difficult with the dates for the Admiral's Cup international offshore teams-racing championship conflicting directly with the America's Cup and few of the proven talented big-boat sailors prepared to spend three or four months on an America's Cup campaign.

In their first two weekends of informal racing in December, Advance at times, was higher than Gretel II but no faster to windward. Downwind,

Advance was higher at times but no faster than Gretel II / BOB ROSS

Advance could hold Gretel II – always fast in this area – and sometimes move away on square runs. On their third weekend of training, Advance was consistently higher and faster than Gretel II, both in the harbour and on a work out into the open sea on a light easterly. Advance was sometimes able to climb dramatically on Gretel II upwind, but mostly they sailed along at the same speed. Advance was out of the water at the end of January to have a new rudder fitted and for alterations to the skeg and bustle area, which that made necessary. Syd Fischer said Advance seemed very good in light and moderate breezes against Gretel II but had a problem in strong breezes which the modification was intended to overcome.

DESIGNER ALAN PAYNE said the rudder would be bigger in area but not much deeper than the skeg to which it was attached. "We certainly have not got the positive knife edge steering control we would like to have. There is always hope in a Twelve Metre that you can get by with a nice little rudder that does not involve much drag. We started off like that but obviously need something bigger. This has shown up particu-

Advance leads Gretel II / BOB ROSS

larly in a breeze." No more ballast could be added because by sinking the boat it would increase the measured waterline length and mean a reduction in sail area, which would improve performance in fresh wind. He added: "But we will not be doing that because whole project is geared to a light to moderate breeze type of boat." Payne said Advance showed promise of living up to his expectations. "There is something good hidden in there somewhere if only we can get it out all the time. Hopefully, improving the steering capabilities will help us."

Meantime Australia II and Challenge 12 in December spent ten days tuning and training off Fremantle which ended with both skippers, John Bertrand (Australia II) and John Savage (Challenge 12) convinced they had the better boat; the hours of straight-line two-boat tuning and the final short match-racing brushes were that close. The preparation of Challenge 12 was delayed by financial

Australia II and Gretel 2 tuning and training off Fremantle, December 1982 / BOB ROSS

Challenge 12 and Australia II, looked evenly matched in the Westpac Series / BOB ROSS

uncertainty until Melbourne businessman Dick Pratt stepped in with a contribution of $300,000, which enabled the Victorian syndicate to settle the debts with the builder of Challenge 12, Steve Ward, designer Ben Lexcen, spar maker Zapspar and the expenses involved in its early sail program.

AUSTRALIA II AND Challenge 12 moved their training and tuning program through January and February to Port Phillip Bay where they operated from a perfect venue at the Royal Yacht Club of Victoria, Williamstown, which was also to be the base for the Westpac Advance Australia Cup series in March. The club installed an hydraulic travel lift and made extra hard-standing available to accommodate the Twelves. The Australia II team lived in the fine old Customs House building next to the club. The Challenge 12 crew also had a live-in situation at the Army's 2nd Commando Company's lines nearby.

"We've got everything here we can expect in Newport, except the Candy Store (a popular Newport restaurant-bar)," said John Longley, veteran crew of all three previous Alan Bond-led challengers and full-time manager of the 1983 challenge from the time the Australia team left Newport in 1980.

Williamstown, the old port suburb of Melbourne, with its blue-stone houses in 1983 was becoming a trendy place. Nelson Place, across from the waterfront, was reminiscent of Newport's Thames Street with a line-up of small restaurants and interesting little pubs including one that featured a mother-and-daughter strip act at lunchtime, which drew heavy

Gretel II, Westpac series, Port Phillip, March 1983 / BOB ROSS

custom from the wharfies. Advance, behind in its preparation, did not make the Westpac series. Gretel II did and although beaten in all but one race, when Challenge 12 was a premature starter and failed to return, was a valuable bench-marker for Australia II and Challenge 12, which in the series of 13 intense match races were almost evenly matched with Australia II winning seven and Challenge 12 five. Challenge 12's crew, skippered by John Savage with Graeme ('Frizzle') Freeman tactician and project manager, snapped together as a unit during the week of racing. They had become completely competitive in the short period (just over three months) they had sailed the boat. Initially they had been greatly helped by the Bond syndicate. Ben Lexcen, designer of both boats, had given them similar rigs and deck plans so sails were swapped in their two-boat tuning programs off Fremantle in December and in Melbourne through January-February. That ecumenical association was completely at an end for the Westpac series; protest flags flew at the hint of a misdemeanour and strong language drifted from the starts to the spectator fleet.

Gretel II was fast in light air / BOB ROSS

Gretel's mainsail was huge / BOB ROSS

GRETEL II WAS well steered by Peter Nicholson with Ingate, helped by the experienced Gerry Garrett, directing a keen young crew. Gretel II had some new sails but they were Dacron, the basic cloth outmoded by the new synthetic materials Kevlar and Mylar and lacked the completely new wardrobe she needed to be an absolute benchmark. But the margins by which she was beaten, over the half-size (12.2n mile) America's Cup style courses, three to four minutes in most races, dispelled Ben Lexcen's recurring nightmare that both boats might be slow. "Before Gordon came down here I was really depressed," said Lexcen after the Westpac series. "I began having second thoughts; maybe I'm mad, maybe they are both a couple of dogs. Gordon did pretty well and I know they are not dogs; they are in the right area."

After one race, in which Gretel II lifted right off Australia II on the beat to the finishing line, Ingate recalls: "Ben was saying that night in front of John Bertrand, 'I am thinking of taking the keel off Australia II.' And Bertrand said, 'Don't do that Ben, it's my problem. I can't steer the boat, I can't keep it on a straight course.' With many more hours on the wheel he finally got to steer it."

The winged keel, always heavily shrouded when the boat was out of the water until after the last race of its dramatic 4-3 America's Cup win over the American defender Liberty, allowed Lexcen to design a light boat with enough stability to go well in a strong breeze and a cutaway profile aft as well as forward and a small keel adding up to improved manoeuvrability. John Bertrand wrote in an article published in Australian Sailing magazine and the US magazine Sail: "Tacking ability was a definite plus. The boat could be tacked from one line to another without having to dip away too much to pick up speed. Compared to a conventional boat like Liberty we could make about 5ft to 10ft a tack whenever we did it right. Australia II was difficult to steer because she does not have a lot of directional stability. Because she does not have a fence or bustle in front of the rudder, is short-keeled and relatively light, she can spin easily. The downside of that is she does not track that easily. The boat has to be trimmed correctly with the sails, otherwise she can be a real bitch to steer."

THE CLOSE DUEL between Australia II and Challenge 12 lifted boats and crews to the level of excellence that eventually won Australia II the America's Cup. Alan Bond at the presentation ceremony for Westpac Advance Australia Cup, said: "We have been racing short courses during the week that tend to amplify the mistakes. I think Australia II just has

Challenge 12 paces Australia II, Westpac series,
Port Phillip, March 1983 / BOB ROSS

Ideal base at the Royal Yacht Club of Victoria, for the three
Twelves – Westpac series, March 1983 / BOB ROSS

the edge and this showed up on the full course. Both boats have lifted; we would not have been as good today without Challenge and Gretel II. We have brought both boats to a new dimension."

Gordon Ingate, who had upstaged everyone by riding backwards and forwards to the club in a white Rolls Royce, loaned from a limousine hire company known to his campaign director Gary Millar, lost his voice immediately he began to speak. He recovered the situation, if not his voice by adding: "I have completely lost my voice by shouting encouragement at my crew, telling them how wonderful they were." He thanked them for, in the terms of the Gretel II slogan, "Advancing Australia's Challenge for the America's Cup."

Ingate watched Australia II win the 1983 America's Cup 4-3 over the American defender Liberty skippered by Dennis Conner, as a guest aboard the New York Yacht Club's VIP spectator motor yacht Scotch Mist. He had joined the club in 1982 at the invitation of Devereaux Barker Junior, who had been chairman of the protest committee in 1970. NYYC member George Carmany, who had known Gordon during the time he spent in Sydney as an American Express executive and sailed a Dragon, seconded him. "I was elected to membership for what they called, 'an international member from Australia' and in 1982, there was only one Australian member, Sir Alexis Albert, because he represented the 1962 challenger as Commodore of the Royal Sydney Yacht Squadron." Around that time, Ingate used to travel to the USA each year to join George Carmany on the New York Yacht Club cruise – a port-hopping series of races along the north-east coast of the USA. He sailed in a record 30 of them until 2016.

As an Australian representative, Ingate reveals, he was at a meeting of the New York Yacht Club's Cup Committee, at the Marble House mansion, on the morning of the first race when there was a strong push led by the secretary of the committee, Victor Romagna, to cancel the race; not because of the club's long campaign challenging the legality of Ben Lexcen's winged keel, but because Alan Bond, would not meet the requirement of the America's Cup Deed of Gift that the challenger would nominate the class of boat and the venue for the next defence if it won. "They invited me to the meeting at nine o'clock and I am hearing for the first time that wanted to cancel the race because Bondy, following the strategy initiated by his syndicate manager Warren Jones of keeping the New York Yacht Club offside, would not tell them in what class and where it would be held if he won. It was done every challenge. I am listening to this going on and said, 'Why are you waiting for Mister Bond to tell you? It's not his challenge. The challenge is between yacht clubs, not individuals. You should be talking to the Commodore of the Royal Perth Yacht Club.' The Cup Committee chairman Bob McCullough said, 'Ingate, you are so right. Why didn't we think of this?' I said, he's got to be in his hotel room' – it was only about quarter past nine – 'See if you can ring him.' They called the Commodore, Peter Dalziel, who said, 'I will be there as soon as I can be. He turned up and said, 'Okay gentlemen, what's the problem?' They told him and he said: 'If we win, we will hold it in Twelve Metres from the Fremantle Sailing Club. If Mister Bond doesn't agree, I will immediately disqualify him from the series. If there is any trouble from Mister Bond, I will wind up his challenge.'"

Ingate's perceived support of the New York Yacht Club in Newport led to a famous clash with Bond. Each race day Ingate would walk down the public dock on which Australia II had its administration office to join Scotch Mist wearing, what Alan Bond believed was a New York Yacht Club cloth hat. One day, according to legend, as Ingate passed, infuriated Bond rushed out and said "Don't you wear that hat on my dock," ripped off the hat, threw it into a puddle of water and jumped up and down on it 18 times. Ingate's version: "It wasn't a New York Yacht Club hat, just an ordinary hat I bought in a local store; its band was about an inch wide where the New York Yacht Club's hat band was about an inch and-half but it was the same colours, red, white and blue. I replied, 'Alan it's not your dock, it's a public dock and this is not a New York Yacht Club hat.' I picked the hat up, it was damp, put it on my head again and walked by. He knew I was a member of the New York Yacht Club and didn't think that I as an Australian was supporting the Australian challenge, which was totally wrong. But I sure wasn't supporting Alan Bond, no question about it."

On returning from Newport, Ingate continued to sail Gretel II in club events and he took the opportunity offered by free shipping to send her to Porto Cervo, Sardinia, for the Twelve Metre world championship in 1984, contested by eight boats, most of them from the 1983 America's Cup line-up, now in Italian ownership. Just getting Gretel II to Porto Cervo, the resort village on a sheltered inlet in the north-eastern tip of Sardinia, became a saga.

"We shipped the boat to Europe, all for free (thanks to Ingate's New York-based shipping line supporter). Franco Biogorno-Nettis the chairman of Transfield – his son Marco was in the crew – came on board as a sponsor," said Ingate. "He knew the people at Alitalia and they helped us to get to Genoa. We were going to go by ship from there to Porto Cervo, with the visiting boats. But the plane broke down in Bombay. The crew walked off because of a pay dispute, leaving us sitting in the middle of the airport. Alitalia put us up in a very poor-standard hotel while they waited for a replacement engine. In the meantime, Gretel II was delivered to Genoa where we were supposed to organise unloading and transfer to another ship for delivery to Sardinia with the other Twelves that were already there.

"By the time we got to Genoa, three days late, the ship had gone so we had to sail Gretel II the 200n miles to Porto Cervo. We had no engine, just a 25hp outboard on a 12ft inflatable dinghy. We left in a beautiful breeze and were sailing well towards Sardinia when the breeze dropped completely and it looked as though we would miss the regatta we had come all this way to attend. We began towing Gretel II with the inflatable but it was very slow; we were lucky to do two knots. Mick York came up the suggestion, 'let's tie the rubber ducky alongside,' and believe it or not, we got it doing five knots that way.

"Very quickly, because we were using so much power, we ran out of fuel approaching Corsica. So, we went into Ajaccio, the port capital of Corsica, which is French territory, with none of the required paperwork; just six of us on board with most of the crew having gone direct to Porto Cervo. We snuck into the port, lucky they didn't pick us up and jail us and got to a place that had fuel. Thank heavens the guy at the fuel depot spoke some English, bought a couple of tins and motored out of the port without anyone else knowing we had been there.

"We finally got to Porto Cervo the day before the first race and away we went in the championship. Our container had been taken on the ship from Genoa with all our spare sails, food and booze. The other boats were all there. Franco had organised quite a big house for us. The Aga Khan welcomed us all with this huge dinner. We had a lot of booze, particularly gin, so we invited all the crews to a welcoming party on the G2. Anyway, the French thought the gin was water and we can remember them pouring out rums and then filling the glasses up with gin because they thought it was water. Did they get drunk? And the next day they were a mess."

Victory '83, the 1983 British America's Cup challenger now owned by a syndicate from the Yacht Club Italiano, skippered by Star sailor Flavio Scala with American Rod Davis, won the opening fleet-racing section of the championship, which seeded the boats for the round robin series. Victory '83 didn't win a race but was consistent with a 3-2-2-3-2 scoreline to finish half a point ahead of Azzura, in the hands of her 1983 America's Cup challenge skipper Mauro Pelaschier. Final placings and points were: 1, Victory '83 (F.Scala, Italy), 3-2-2-3-2, 27 points; 2, Azzura (M.Pelaschier, Italy) 4-5-1-1-4, 26.5; 3, Freedom (D.Conner, USA), 1-3-8-4-5, 23.25; 4, Canada 1 (T.McLaughlin, Canada), 7-1-5-2-6, 22.15; 5, Challenge 12 (J.Savage, Italy), 8-4-6-5-1, 20.25; 6, New Zealand (C.Dickson, New Zealand), 6-6-3-6-3, 18; 7, France 3 (B.Mosbacher, USA), 2-8-7-7-7, 13; 8, Gretel II (G.Ingate, Australia), 5-7-4-ret-8, 12.

For the match racing, Victory '83, Freedom, Challenge 12 and France 3, formed division one while Azzura faced Canada 1, New Zealand and Gretel II in division two. When Bob Mosbacher (brother of Bus) and Buddy Melges returned to the United States after the fleet racing, leaving France 3 without an afterguard and about to be withdrawn from the regatta, Ingate offered to skipper France 3 and raised $10,000 at a dinner at the Costa Smeralda Yacht Club to keep her racing. He handed Gretel II over to Graham Newland for the rest of the regatta. He assembled a polyglot crew with a nucleus of the Frenchmen that had been sailing on the boat, one or two of the Gretel II support team, Jorg Diesch, the German Olympic gold medallist in the Flying Dutchman class, who was holidaying in Porto Cervo after the Sardinia Cup series and Bob Fisher, the British yachting journalist.

"The boat was crewed by Baron Bich's crew from the 1983 America's Cup who had hired the boat but ran out of money. The guy who had organised it had to go back to France. The crew and boat were there in going order so I said I would skipper it to keep them going in the regatta. In one race, it blew like the clappers out there in the waters off Porto Cervo and we were heading for Italy. I thought, 'If we go head to wind we will lose this mainsail for sure, it was flapping so hard.' We were in a lot of difficulty; the boat was taking on a lot of water and the bilge pumps weren't working. I didn't want to be on board a Twelve Metre while it's sinking. The squall went through, it lasted about two or three hours and it finally dropped off and we got back to port."

Ingate said the regatta, in spectacular surroundings and with a vibrant social scene had been a worthwhile experience, the best being beating Freedom sailed by Dennis Conner during the fleet racing in light weather. "When he couldn't beat Gretel II he just packed his bag and went home. That's when we realised Gretel II was a bloody good boat. The mainsail

France 3 and Gretel II, 1984 Twelve Metre Worlds, Sardinia / INGATE FAMILY ARCHIVE

was huge and the whole story of my time with Gretel II would have different if we had made it reefable. Alan Payne reckoned the mast would break in heavy weather if the main was reefed. It was just terrible"

Start Twelve Metre world championship, Fremantle, December 1986. Gretel II heads right early, her Dacron sails showing out in the bunch / BOB ROSS

France 3 and Gretel II were both eliminated in the preliminary rounds of the match-racing. Victory '83 eventually won the final match-racing series by three races to one over Azzura.

INGATE, BACK IN Australia sought testimonials from designers Alan Payne and Ben Lexcen to Gretel II's ongoing suitability as a benchmark for 1987 America's Cup defenders. Payne said that with the Cup races to be sailed in an area of strong winds, Gretel II would not be competitive but could easily be made so by adding ballast. 'However, Gretel II will not then meet the requirements of the 12 Metre rule and will have become a '12½ Metre' or a '13 Metre.' This should not matter for trial horse sailing.

"It is assumed that she would be given new sails equal to those of her opponents. It is also assumed that the masts and spars, her rigging and her hull would be maintained in good condition, able to take the bigger loads resulting from the increased ballast. The manoeuvring abilities of Gretel II, while much less than those of Australia II, are like those of Courageous and Liberty. This being so, I believe she can serve well as a training yacht in matters of racing tactics as well as of straight-line speed."

Lexcen's testimonial concluded that Gretel II was an excellent training vessel for Twelve Metre crews. "Over half of Australia II's Cup-winning crew began their Twelve Metre careers on Gretel II; John Bertrand as a sail trimmer in 1970. However, the main advantage is that its classic hull form, together with the benefits accruing from the 'grandfather' rule, means that it can be used as a competitive benchmark for a new

Italia leads first reach stack-up, Twelve Metre worlds / KAORU SOEHATA

vessel to be constructed to the rules in force for the America's Cup in 1987. At times in the past her usefulness as a trial horse, for reasons of expediency, politics and simply poor management, has not been fully exploited. Given a commitment to replace her outdated sails and properly maintain and crew her, Gretel II can still play a constructive role in a successful Twelve Metre campaign. All the tank-testing technology etc. (while all necessary), cannot replace the benefits to be gained from racing and sailing competitively two Twelve Metres side by side. To avoid the risks of building new boats together (my concern about such risks associated with Australia II's campaign were only dispelled when both Challenge 12 and Australia II raced Gretel II in March 1983), I would recommend to any intending syndicate the value of Gretel II.

"I believe that her value may be further increased by moving the rig and mast up to 0.5m aft, thereby increasing the size of the J (headsail measurement) and decreasing the area of the mainsail, thereby increasing tacking performance and ability to windward. The area lost in the mainsail would in fact be made up by the developments of modern technology and materials and sail-making techniques."

Ingate still believed Gretel II was a valuable benchmark in light weather and was disappointed that Alan Payne would not consider putting a reefing provision into her huge mainsail because he believed it could break the mast. He sent her to Fremantle for the Twelve Metre world fleet racing championship in 1986. "We wanted to help ensure that the America's Cup remained in Australia. We went over on the basis that we would get some races in with the light easterly in the morning and if it stayed in all day we would win. We got a lot of help from the locals who had befriended us when we returned from the world championship in England, in 1979 and match-raced against Australia. 'A local fisherman said, 'Do you want somewhere to live Gordon, you and your crew?'

"'How much housing do you want? Fourteen crew; number so and so street; it's all ready for you'; unbelievable.

"'Do you want a boat to go around with your boat? Yes, done.'

"'Do you want a car to drive around in? Done.'"

AFLOAT IT WAS different story with Gretel II outclassed in a strong fleet of 14 including eight new boats warming up for the 1987 America's Cup off Fremantle. Australia III (Colin Beashel) won from New Zealand KZ 5 (Chris Dickson) with America II (John Kolius) third. Gretel II finished last. "We had one light race the whole of the series," said Ingate. "It was just terrible."

By then Ingate was member of the board of Governors of the Sydney Heritage Fleet, a division of the Australian National Maritime Museum on Darling Harbour Sydney. "I realised if I donated the boat to the museum I could get a tax deduction and that was the way to go because organising a crew to keep her going every Saturday was getting very difficult. One of the things that prompted me to do it, I put the word around that if any young people wanted to come for a sail on a Twelve Metre I would be only too happy to take them out for the day. I had to put a special mooring down for her in Neutral Bay. When this young fellow was getting down into the club tender and I happened to step down onto the tender at the same time, he said, 'Excuse me Mister Ingate, who

Gretel II with a youthful crew on Sydney Harbour towards
the end of Ingate's ownership / INGATE ARCHIVE

pays me for today's outing?'

"I said, 'Where did you get the information that we were paying you to come sailing?'

"He said, 'Everyone gets paid to go sailing on a Twelve Metre; they're professional sailors and that's what I am building up to. I believe I am entitled to a day's pay.'

"I said, 'The boat is now for sale.' That really did upset me.

"The day I delivered the boat to the museum I steered her there in the morning and skippered my daughter Christine's Yngling in a harbour race in the afternoon."

11

NEW YORK YC AND ROYAL SYDNEY YS CRUISES

GORDON INGATE COMBINED HIS LOVE of sailing and socialising by competing in 30 New York Yacht Club annual cruises and 42 Royal Sydney Yacht Squadron annual cruises. The New York Yacht Club Cruise, a port-hopping combination of racing and cruising, was the club's initial event at its founding in 1814 when six yachts sailed from The Battery in New York city to Newport, Rhode Island, with overnight stops at Huntington on Long Island, New Haven, Gardner's Bay and Oyster Point.

The Royal Sydney YS cruise, over four days each Easter, was inspired by the experiences of crew members of Gretel during Australia's first America's Cup challenge in 1962, who sailed aboard Gretel's trial horse Vim in the New York Yacht Club Cruise that year with four American Twelves: Nefertiti, Weatherly, Columbia and Easterner. Crew member Mick York described that cruise in Royal Sydney YS's 1862-2000 history:

"On Monday, July 30, we started in Vim in the New York Yacht Club Cruise and I was lucky enough to be selected in her crew, whilst the other members spent the week working on alterations to Gretel. (Note: the challenging syndicate had decided that Gretel would not sail against any American Twelves before the actual Cup races).

"We had chartered an 85ft cruiser, fully equipped with skipper, cook, steward and deck hand. We would eat and sleep on this cruiser and with her and our tender Offsider we set off. Our first race was a downhill gybing duel and we finished up in fourth place, being beaten by Nefertiti, Weatherly and Columbia and coming in ahead of Easterner. This race finished at a place called Wattapoisett, in Buzzard's Bay, about 40 miles from Newport. That evening, several of the 160 vessels in the cruise tied together and we were invited aboard Cotton Blossom and Windigo for cocktails. It is hard to describe the condition of the yachts in these races, as without seeing them, you could not believe it. There would be very few under 40ft and most ranged from 50ft to 100ft and some over this. Many of them have at least two paid hands, a skipper and deck-hand-cum-steward and many have up to five paid hands. The varnish and woodwork are like any grand piano.

"Well, back to sailing. The next race was a triangular course finishing at Marion; we were again placed fourth, being beaten by Weatherly, Columbia and Easterner and coming in ahead of Nefertiti. The following day we fell back to fifth place. This race finished at Woods Hole where we were invited on board the Mercers' motor yacht Blue Jacket. She is 110ft long and carries a crew of seven – captain, mate, engineer, cook, two deck hands and a steward. She is carpeted throughout and has many large staterooms, having their own bathrooms etc, is fully air conditioned and equipped with all the latest in radio telephones, radar, automatic pilot; in fact, I believe six tons of wiring. Mr Mercer is a shipping magnate whose company runs 120 ships. He also owns Weatherly.

"In the race the following day, we improved considerably and finished in third place, beating Easterner and Nefertiti. The race finished at New Bedford, where a dinner was arranged. Saturday 4th dawned a beautiful day and we got away to a good start. We had a few lucky breaks and took advantage of them to come in second, being beaten by 1min 40sec by Easterner. At the end of this race we were still 40 miles from Newport so, as the wind was light, we picked up a tow from Offsider and arrived back at Newport about 8pm."

Gretel squad member Brian Northam, who had been aboard Vim

for the Cruise, enjoyed it so much that on his return he prompted the Royal Sydney Yacht Squadron to conduct something similar over the Easter weekend with the major point score trophy to be the New York Yacht Club Cup, a trophy which had been presented to the RSYS by the Commodore of the NYYC, Percy Chubb II, during a visit to Sydney with his wife as a memento of the 1962 America's Cup campaign, which the NYYC thought had been conducted in the spirit of friendship and good sportsmanship. "It's a huge beer mug," said Ingate. "If anyone wins it three times they will keep it and the NYYC will supply another one. I have won it twice."

Ingate sailed on the inaugural RSYS cruise in 1970 with his offshore racer Caprice of Huon. Bill Northam, Caprice's former owner and father of the Cruise founder Brian Northam, was Cruise Captain. A fleet of 37 yachts, including RSYS Commodore Richard Dickson's Eight Metre Norske, started on the morning of Saturday, May 9 for the first stopover, in Careel Bay, Pittwater; about 20 nautical miles away. "We had a big left-over sea from a sou'-easter, which had moderated after blowing for several days," Ingate said. "To keep out of the current I took Caprice inshore and was leading the fleet when I saw these big waves ahead of us. So, I sharpened up and sailed out past where I had seen this huge wave lining up off Long Reef.

"Looking back and there is Donald Maclurcan sailing his little boat Morag Bheag and I thought, 'Jesus, he is too close.' This big wave loomed up and he is between Long Reef and this wave. I thought, 'Wow, there's going to be some problems here.' The wave broke ten feet above him; it didn't wash him onto the reef, it might have been a few yards; but the boat heeled over completely, covered in water, swamped; they disappeared completely."

The RSYS history records that a short race for lady helms followed on Sunday. The next offshore race of the Cruise, from Pittwater to Moon Islet, half a mile to the east of the entrance to Lake Macquarie, started but ran out of wind and with the yachts still only off Cape Three Points, was abandoned. The yachts proceeded to Lake Macquarie under power. The fleet raced on Lake Macquarie on Tuesday and returned to Pittwater on Wednesday, racing from Wybung Head to Careel Bay. Thursday's race for the Club Captain's trophy was sailed on Pittwater and on Friday the race went to Refuge Bay.

"When we got to Lake Macquarie old man Dicko (RSYS Commodore Richard Dickson) took control," said Ingate. "We spent a lot of time at the Wangi Workers' Club, a haven for fishermen and yachties, where there is waterfrontage for 15 or 20 yachts and that was the start of the New York Yacht Club style cruise. The one big difference was the Squadron allowed us to take children; the New York Yacht Club didn't, maybe because of the amount of booze that was being drunk." In later cruises, the Squadron encouraged boat owners to take youngsters from its youth training program. Besides gaining some offshore experience, they got to know older members of the club.

Another memorable incident from the early days of the RSYS Cruise with Caprice of Huon was in a strong south-sou'-easter. "We went over the top of a pretty steep following wave and as we came down, the boat took off," said Ingate. "I looked up and the spinnaker was above the mast; the halyard had enough stretch left in it. The spinnaker then came down and collapsed on top of the Brookes & Gatehouse wind instruments. One of the young blokes went up on the spare halyard and could free the spinnaker but the Brookes & Gatehouse gear was completely buggered and the Royal Sydney Yacht Squadron burgee had disappeared."

The RSYS Cruises Ingate enjoyed most were the earlier ones south to Port Kembla and Port Hacking but rates as by far the best, one to Lake Macquarie, organised by Cruise Captain Charles Maclurcan, in 1974. The RSYS history records that the fleet totalled 70 yachts and seven motor cruisers: "A combination of a soft south-westerly and flooding tide brought the race to a halt not far from the middle of the Heads. It was some time before a gentle nor'-easter allowed the fleet to sail slowly northward, so slowly that it was evident as the afternoon progressed that the leaders could not make Pittwater before the time limit. The race was shortened at Hole in the Wall and the boats motored to a rendezvous at the Basin in Pittwater.

"There was a ladies' day race on a warm and sunny Sunday and that evening a barbecue was held at The Basin and all participants had an early night as there was to be a pre-dawn rendezvous before the long race to Moon Islet (just off the entrance to Lake Macquarie).

"As early morning fog gave way to a balmy autumn day, lack of wind forced the fleet to motor to Norah Head before the race could start. Luckily the breeze then gained strength and an enjoyable race was held over the last ten miles of the passage to Moon Islet. The fleet entered Lake Macquarie through the sometimes-difficult passage at Swansea and was securely moored at the Wangi District Workers' Club jetties before sunset, where an informal welcoming dance was held. Despite having been awake from the small hours, many hardy sailors enjoyed the evening thoroughly.

"The balmy autumn weather continued on the Tuesday and a course around the northern end of the lake provided a testing race. The earlier leaders had sailed impeccably and appeared assured of victory until an incoming nor'-easter found them on the wrong side of the course, allowing the middle markers to snatch the lead in a very close finish. All the yachts met at Lake Macquarie Yacht Club for drinks and a buffet dinner afterwards.

"The next day, Wednesday, was a lay day and a bus tour of the Hunter Valley vineyards with a barbecue lunch had been arranged so nearly everybody headed inland for what proved to be a very enjoyable tour. The bus parties returned to Wangi in time for a dinner dance at the Wangi Wangi RSL Club. A splendid dinner with good music providing a fitting finale to a merry day.

"The glorious weather ended on the Thursday as rain brought some wind with it at last. The smaller boats were pleased that this gave them a chance of a better showing. Despite the rain, the now traditional barbecue at Rathmines was held with undiminished quality and much gaiety. The rain continued through until next morning when another early rendezvous took place for the exit through the Swansea Channel. It was damp and uninspiring and a moderate southerly was blowing. The cruise officials took that into account and with a forecast for easing conditions, decided to race. Unfortunately, the forecast of easing conditions was only too accurate and only two of the yachts were able to finish in time at Refuge Bay. The next day the southerly was still blowing and had increased somewhat so that the final race from Refuge Bay to Careel Bay was completed in record time."

Not all the cruises have ended that happily. The RYSYS history records: "A yacht which had ignored the Cruise Captain's advice and left Lake Macquarie in the face of a severe south-easterly gale was lost on Cape Three Points and three people died." That year, Ingate remembers leaving the boat at the Lake and catching the train home. "That put a damper not only on the cruise but people just cruising up and down the NSW coast," he said. "Remember, the Tasman Sea can be wild."

Ingate reckons that the earlier cruises south carried less risk. "I was perfectly happy to go to Botany Bay, Port Kembla or Wollongong so that you could come back safely in a nor'easter, a westerly or even a hard southerly. But coming back from Lake Macquarie in a hard southerly

Raft up in Pittwater, 2003 RSYS Cruise / INGATE FAMILY ARCHIVE

put a damper on it, plus crossing the bar although now the bar is fully dredged so big boats can go in and out. They do invite the motor yachts to turn up as they should. They can be very helpful at times for yachts in trouble."

After he sold Caprice of Huon in 1975, Ingate continued sailing in the cruise, on other people's boats and a Warwick Hood designed 40-footer called Nina, which he owned for eight years. The boat was originally owned by Sir Alexis Albert, the second of his yachts named Norn. The first was a classic Eight Metre designed by Johan Anker of Norway. Norn II was one four yachts that sailmaker Peter Cole had commissioned to a Warwick Hood design with the aim of starting a class. Ingate relates how he purchased her in the 1960s, in unusual circumstances:

"I am sitting at home one day when the 'phone rings.

"'Lex Albert here Gordon, I want you to buy my boat.'

"At this stage, I had Gretel II, Caprice of Huon, a 5.5 and a Dragon. I needed another boat like a hole in the head.

"'I would be honoured, you've got a beautiful boat and I would like to own it.'

"So, I ring my favourite partner in crime, Mrs Saalfeld and told her about it and she said, 'Oh yeah let's buy it.' I bought it. Sir Alexis said, 'The one thing I am keeping is the name', which went back a long way.

"I called the boat Nina after my mother-in-law Mrs Saalfeld. My mother got very upset because I didn't call it Greta, her name, because Greta didn't sound like a good a name for a boat. From the time I got her, she was just a beautiful boat to sail. We made her go a bit better than Sir Alexis did, got some new sails and the big thing I did – the spinnaker had been flown from the hounds position on the mast so you could only carry a small spinnaker. I recut some old Twelve Metre spinnakers and flew them from the masthead. I put a stronger backstay on and made sure I only carried those spinnakers dead square downwind and in under 15 knots of breeze and nothing could touch us."

AFTER HE SOLD Nina eight years later, Ingate chartered boats for the cruise. For the 2003 Cruise he chartered the Sydney 38 Wadadli

Sydney 38 Wadadli, chartered for the 2003 Squadron Cruise / INGATE FAMILY ARCHIVE

Ingate family members of all ages manned Wadadli
INGATE FAMILY ARCHIVE

(named after a beer from the West Indies) with a team of ten Ingates including his six grandsons. He also chartered a 42ft Catalina Symphony as mother ship to accommodate all in comfort at Cruise stopovers. The team was: Gordon (Skip), 77, skipper and helm; Stephen (son), 47, bowman; Nicholas (grandson), 18, trimmer; Timothy (grandson), 16, grinder and trimmer; Jonathon (grandson), 12, spinnaker packer; C.C

Young Wingate family members crewed Soundtrack on the
2005 RSYS Cruise / INGATE FAMILY ARCHIVE

(grandson), 10, spinnaker packer; Christine (daughter), 47, guy trimmer and crew boss; Jason (grandson), 18, mainsheet; Josh (grandson), 16, mastman; Gabrielle (daughter-in-law), Blythe Spirit tender driver; Margaret Hearder, 'ageless, tenderer to all'.

Ingate chartered the J35 Sound Track from Tim Cox for the 2005 and 2006 Squadron Cruises. A chartered houseboat provided accommodation for up to ten family members – children and grandchildren – and friends. He was back again in 2010 and 2011, in Minerva, a DK43 also chartered from Tim Cox.

Adults enjoy the hospitality on the chartered houseboat, 2005 RSYS Cruise
INGATE FAMILY ARCHIVE

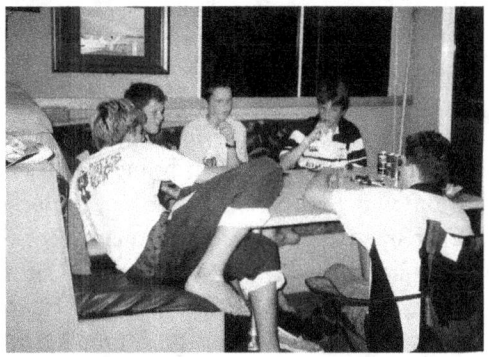

The youngsters play poker
INGATE FAMILY ARCHIVE

"Minerva was difficult to control downwind with a spinnaker so we moved the pole forward and sheeted the kicker down hard to muzzle the spinnaker and avoid it gyrating the boat. I do that on the Dragon when I'm having trouble controlling it downwind in fresh breezes."

Ingate remembers the last cruise he did, with Minerva, because he was poised to win the New York Yacht Club Cup for the third time and so keep it. "We were manoeuvring for the start off Barrenjoey in a 15-knot sou-'easter, which would have suited us for the work back to Sydney with a finish in Watsons Bay, when a bad repair on the mainsail failed and a seam let go. We didn't have any way of repairing it so we motored home. It was a big disappointment for me because I understand we would have kept the trophy. I think that was the last cruise I did. I was getting a little bit older and the children were doing their own thing. I thought 42 cruises was a fair time to go."

RSYS committee boat Gitana, after getting the fleet away on
Lake Macquarie, 2003 Cruise / INGATE FAMILY ARCHIVE

INGATE'S FIRST NEW York Yacht Club Cruise was in 1979 on Arcadia, Bob Stone's 69ft McCurdy and Rhodes design, before Stone became Commodore of the New York Yacht Club. Stone, who died in 2006, was a charismatic figure, well remembered for the grace and humour with which he handed over the America's Cup to the Australians in 1983. "The cruise went to Maine that year. His crew had been sailing with him for years and we had a great time. I had met Bob Stone in 1977 and through him got introduced to the New York Yacht Club community."

BACK IN 1982, he was crewing on Curt C, a 60ft motor yacht owned by Bill Packer. The first boat Ingate chartered for the cruise was a New York 36, Slippery Sam, in 1983. His son Stephen and daughter-in-law Gabrielle went with him. "Eight of us slept on board," Ingate said. "That was an exciting cruise because we were on a very small boat and we were doing very well on handicap. We were going from Woods Hole in the Cape Cod area across Buzzards Bay to Pandaram Harbour, New Bedford. We were about half way across Buzzards Bay when Gabrielle says:

"'Gee whizz. Do you expect anybody to be out here, calling out?'

"And I said, 'No way, it's a seagull.'

"She said, 'I can hear a person calling for help.'

"And I said, 'Come on, there's nobody out here.'

"She said, 'Okay, everybody keep quiet' – they were all talking – and we all kept quiet; there was no doubt about it; a human voice calling for help. We couldn't see any boats.

New York Yacht Club annexe, Harbour Court, Newport
INGATE FAMILY ARCHIVE

NYYC Cruise boats assembled off the clubhouse / INGATE FAMILY ARCHIVE

"'Where do you think the voices are coming from, Gabes?'

"'Over there,'

"So, we headed over there and there's two blokes in the water. They were Portuguese crewmen off a ship in the port we were going to and they were 15 miles offshore, to go fishing, in a tinny they had hired, which sank. They were about to go down; they were buggered. We hauled them on board and finished the race, which was the fastest way of getting there and delivered them to an ambulance when we reached port. They couldn't speak English but were very effusive in expressing, 'thank you for saving our lives.'

"That was the second-last day of the cruise. We stayed there that night and sailed back to Newport the next day to see the America's Cup.'

In 1986, Ingate joined the NYYC Cruise again, unexpectedly:
"I am sitting here at home, the telephone rings.

"'Bob Stone here.'

"'What can I do for you?'

"'I want you to come over and skipper Anitra. Her owner, my best friend, has just died and the family wants to go on the cruise.'

"'Wow, that's a pretty big ask, Bob.'

"'You CAN do it, come over.'

"It was a beautiful boat, an S&S 55-footer, all varnished. It was fantastic and a big year; we did very well with her."

In 1987, Ingate invited Ted Kaufman, the Sydney offshore owner-skipper, to join him in chartering a boat for the cruise. "I chartered a motor-sailer, Lorna D, the only boat I could find, which turned out to be a useful choice for the cruise that year was in Maine where the currents are strong. I said, 'We will be able to pick up a crew. Okay Ted, I will meet you on a certain date and a certain time at Brooklin in Maine.' Do you know where Ted ended up? At Brooklyn in Seattle, the whole width of the country from where he should have been. So, I am at Maine airport waiting for him to come in on the flight. When he wasn't on it, I called him: 'Don't tell me you're in Brooklyn, Seattle.'

"'Yes, that's where I am.'

"He arrived in Maine two days later so we had to catch the cruise up."

Ingate asked Kaufman to do the navigating. "I should not have asked him because his method of navigating was plus or minus five degrees where it should have been two degrees in Maine where there are bloody rocks everywhere, the currents are so strong and the passages are so narrow. Anyway, we had a good time. Their lay day featured a lobster bake, professionally organised."

He was back in 1988 with the NY36, Turning Point and in 1989 with Singoalla, one of the New York 40 one-designs owned by Larry Lavers, the first of seven Ingate sailed aboard or

Gordon and Margaret, Judy and George Carmany / NYYC

The J44 Stampede, which Ingate chartered, on the 2008 NYYC Cruise
DAN NERNEY / NYYC

chartered for the cruise. The NY40 was to become his favoured boat on the cruise because of the close quality of the class racing within the broader mixed fleets and the companionship of the crews. The New York Yacht Club initiated the class of 40ft Doug Peterson-designed boats in the 1970s and its fleet reached a total of 21 boats. Sometimes Ingate sailed on NY40s owned by, or in joint charters with, George Carmany, his friend from Dragon-sailing days when Carmany, an executive with American Express, was stationed in Sydney.

AFTER THEY SAILED the 1990 and 1991 cruises on Tom Gill's J44 Night Moves, in 1992 Ingate and Carmany chartered the J35 Seawind. "The most exciting thing; George was steering going up towards the finishing line in Maine," said Ingate. "We are on starboard tack; I am down to leeward trimming the genoa and suddenly, I see this cruising boat coming towards us on port tack. I thought, "He doesn't know the rules, he is going to collide with us."

"I said, 'Christ, George, we should tack.'

"George said, 'I don't want to tack, I am aiming at the finishing line.'

"I grabbed the tiller and hauled it up like buggery.

"And George was terribly upset, you couldn't blame him, he couldn't see this boat coming and anyway we turned and it went under us. And

New York 40 with modest tender / DAN NERNEY / NYYC

George said, 'Gee that was close.'

"I got my voice back.

"I'd pulled the tiller so hard, I broke it. We finished the race but on the strength of it, the crew of the J35 had three new tillers made and gave one to George and one to me. It's still hanging up downstairs."

INGATE AND CARMANY again joined forces to charter Park Benjamin's NY40 Gambler for the 1993 Cruise, which was in Maine. During the cruise they hit a rock, damaging the rudder and keel. The NY40 class history records: "They found so many rocks that Gordon Ingate became known as 'Gordons on the rocks,' after the gin." Carmany liked the boat so much that he immediately bought her from Benjamin with the purchase price absorbing the cost of the repairs; about US$5,000 worth. They had the rudder repaired overnight and went racing next day. Carmany changed the boat's name to Hornet and Ingate joined him for the 1994 Cruise on her.

Ingate has a vivid memory of hitting a rock in the 1994 Cruise. "I was on the toilet, with my wet weather pants around my knees when George hits a rock. The boat stops and the contents of the toilet comes up and goes all over me. Gee I was a mess. We had a 60ft mother ship called Windflower, crewed by a husband and wife team, who looked after us beautifully after each race."

"In 1997, we chartered a Swan 40 called Ugly Duckling. The owner

NY40 Taniwha (left) winning the Una Cup, 2004 NYYC Cruise
DAN NERNEY / NYYC

had done a fantastic job of getting the best possible rating, much as Graham Newland did with Caprice of Huon and with Andy McGowan on board we did remarkably well."

Ingate returned to the New York 40s, chartering Altair from Struther Scott, for the 1998 Cruise, to Maine that year and in 1999, to Boston, with Sydney friend Bill Manning and Andy McGowan again. In 2000 he joined Tom Gill, who had sold his J44, on Gill's brand new 65-footer Anthem, which Gill and his wife were to sail around the world. "The cruise went to New York City, from Newport to East River, up Long Island Sound and back to Newport. The wind just disappeared because

Taniwha, fully crewed, in a mark rounding, Una Cup / DAN NERNEY / NYYC

of the high-rise buildings in Manhattan and there was lots of current."

For the 2002 he chartered the J46 Sonnenschein; "A great boat. Judy Claggert, Tom Claggert's eldest daughter in an extremely wealthy family, who had looked after us very well at the 1977 America's Cup, hired a 110ft motor cruiser and became our mother ship." He was back in 2003

Taniwha sailed the long races in 2004 with a crew of only four
INGATE FAMILY ARCHIVE

with the NY40 Altair, which he had chartered for the third time, with Tony and Cindy Hearder on board. "That was fantastic." They had a very wild ride on the Plymouth to Salem leg: "We rounded up a couple of times; poor Cindy had never been on a boat laying on its ear, but I knew that sooner or later she would come up again."

IN 2004 INGATE won the Una Cup, a round-the-buoys race for New York 40s in the cruise at Newport, with Taniwha. For the passage races he sailed with only four crew members. "You can race the 40s with a lot less crew. There were only four of us on board – myself and Margaret, Tim and Colleen Jermain – and it was great fun but hard work, particularly gybing the spinnaker with only four on board against boats with eight. We pushed hard with no problems."

Gordon with the Una Cup, the NYYC's fourth oldest trophy / DAN NERNEY / NYYC

Ingate chartered Sonnenschein again for the 2005 Cruise, in Maine that year, with Sydney sailing friends Leon Cremer, Doug Sturrock and their wives and a motor-sailer as mother ship.

THERE WERE PROBLEMS for Ingate on the 2010 Cruise when he chartered the 50ft ketch Lone Fox and ended up in court. "The owner, who was the navigator, should have known better than to put me on the rocks. He reckoned that I put him on the rocks. He wanted to sue me for the cost of the boat plus more. After two years in the courts, he didn't win, we didn't win either; the only winners in the American system are the lawyers."

Post-race party time NYYC Cruise / DAN NERNEY / NYYC

He chartered a classic yacht called Black Watch, designed by Olin Stephens not long after his famous 52ft yawl Dorade, for the 2011 Cruise and in 2012 a very slow Ted Hood cruiser called Wanderer with Tony and Cindy Hearder on board. "We entered her in the racing division but we were finishing an hour behind the last boat. In 2013, we were on a 75ft motor yacht called M4, in super luxury but after the end of the cruise, Margaret was taken to hospital."

Ingate sailed the New York Yacht Club Cruise for the last time in 2016, without his soul-mate Margaret Hearder, on a 'slow, old boat.' Margaret had died on April 22, 2015. "It was terrible without her," he said.

12

INTO FARMING

GORDON INGATE'S GOOD FORTUNE CONTINUED into a new career in 1976, into farming, based on the Tea Gardens district of north-eastern New South Wales, inspired by moves into the rural scenario by some of his sailing businessmen friends. In 2019 he was still buying properties and by then owned seven and had six to eight employees involved mainly in growing Wagyu beef cattle.

"I had been in engineering all my life and I thought it was time to get my hands dirty with dirt, rather than grease and oil."

His wife Sally had a friend, Judy Pitt of the agricultural family company Pitt and Sons, on a property near Wellington, NSW. The Ingates used to visit the Pitts and became more and more interested in farming lifestyle. But Wellington was a five-hour drive from Sydney in those days.

Then a new opportunity came to Ingate when he was invited out for a sail on Sir Robert Crichton-Brown's ocean racer Balandra. There, he met David Williams who had been hired by W.R. Carpenter, mortgagee

The farmhouse at Tara, where Gordon resides / GORDON INGATE

in possession of a pine forest at Tea Gardens, to sell various properties off the books. "He told his friends he could get properties at much less than their market value because all the mortgagee in possession wants is his money back; he is not interested in making a profit."

Ingate went to Tea Gardens, looked at a 1,000-acre property that Williams wanted to sell, but found it was covered with pine trees, an average 860 trees to the acre, that had failed. "They should never have been planted in the first place because the soil was very poor. I bought it very cheaply with these small pine trees on it."

Ingate did manage to sell some of the trees to an American firm building children's playgrounds using small diameter pine trees. "They needed a four-inch tree for supporting structures. Because the trees were old, they were incredibly strong in compression. We started selling them to mines; much lighter and easier to carry down the mine for props."

He sold more to sailing farmer friends Graham Newland and Ted Kaufman for fence posts. "I realised they still had value so I had the property insured. I got a cover note on it. Given the condition of the trees, the policy should never have been issued.

Tara vista with the dam full / GORDON INGATE

"On the 17th of December 1979, the biggest bush fire started in the area and burnt down 14,000 acres of pine trees and the only owner insured was Gordon Ingate, so a lot of people said, 'he started the bush fire.'

"I made the insurance claim and they paid

it. They found the guy who admitted starting the fire. They wanted to send him to jail but he was mongoloid and they didn't.

"So, I started to clean it up and buy other properties in the area because I realised it was a growth area, although totally wrong for pine trees."

The cattle are healthy / GORDON INGATE

"Because of the fire, another rainbow popped out of my arse. David Williams, who had been in Japan trying to sell the pine trees for wood chips, secured an order for 50,000 tonnes of the chips for making paper.

"So Johnny Keon and David Williams bought a chipping mill. We had to get the burnt trees down and chipped within six months because if they are still standing and the top is burnt, the sap runs down the tree and the tree loses its strength. Forty foresters worked 24 hours a day, seven days a week, to get the trees knocked down.

"Word came back that carbon was getting into the chips. We began water blasting the chips, sent them off to Japan and the word came back, 'They are the best chips we have ever had. They are completely clean, please carry on with the 50,000 tonnes.'"

Keon and Williams had to stop after chipping 25,000 tons when the operation became uneconomical with the trees broken up into small pieces. They had to buy 25,000 tons of chipped pine trees on the open world market to fulfil the contract. They sold the water blasting machinery to a company in South Australia that had had massive fire in its pine forest.

Ingate cleaned up the Tea Gardens property and realising it was in a growth area, bought nearby properties. He uses them to grow Wagyu beef cattle. "I started buying Poll Herefords but they were too close to the coast and suffered terribly from foot rot. Wagyu cattle are better for a wet climate."

Gordon inspects a fence / GORDON INGATE

Gordon employs six to eight helpers
GORDON INGATE

The rainbows continued. "Two years ago, Chinese drove up to the Nerong Park property in a big black limousine and said, 'Do you mind if we give you a price?' They gave me a figure way above market value; I was astounded by it and said, 'You've just bought yourself a cattle property.'

"The Chinese took control of the cattle property, paid me in Australian dollars, which I am still enjoying. With their money I bought other properties."

Why does he tackle the long weekly commute drive between Tea Gardens and Cowdroy Avenue? "It gives me an interest, something to think about, keeps me active. I come back on Thursday nights and do some things with my helpers on Fridays before sailing on Saturdays.

"It's keeping me alive."

The farm workers start at seven each morning. Gordon has a meeting with them around eight; though not every day, and then drives around in a utility he keeps at Tea Gardens, checking on what is happening around the various properties: "Checking fences, what needs ploughing, what needs slashing and doing the rain dance. We haven't had any useful rain since before Christmas (he said towards the end of February, 2019), which is unusual for my properties because they are right on the coast at the entrance to Port Stephens.

"On Wednesday night it rained hard and we had 44mm, which is just fantastic. It filled all the small dams up but it hasn't softened the ground. Because it was heavy it ran off the hard ground into the dams but didn't soften the soil so the root systems of the grass still need moisture; at least two inches. That's going to make the hay grow and the price might come down in the local area. The haymakers are making too much money because of the drought; they can sell the hay at whatever price they like."

Ingate plays bridge on Monday nights, gets invited out to dinner by various friends but otherwise his social life is centred on Sydney.

13

BACK TO THE DRAGONS

GORDON INGATE RETURNED TO THE Dragon class in 1994 when he bought Taranui from Peter Morris, son of his former 5.5 metre and offshore crew-mate and friend Mick Morris. Peter had purchased Taranui from her Canadian owner while competing in the world championship at Vancouver in 1983, as mainsheet hand for Sydney skipper Ross Stiffe, with Gary Taylor for'ard, on the chartered boat Obsession, to finish second to local boat Mistral (Bob Burgess) while another Sydney crew, headed by Jamie Wilmot on the chartered Sunkist was third. Obsession won the Canadian championship preceding the worlds. The fleet was a hot one including the current world champion Marcus Glas, who finished fourth, and European champion Horst Strohe.

Marty Godsil of Seattle, who built Taranui in 1980, introduced some cost-saving measures that did not meet class rules. "The fibreglass hull instead of having a thickness of 3/8in had two 3/16in skins with a balsa

Taranui heads upwind, 1996 Prince Philip Cup, Sydney Harbour / BOB ROSS

core in between which made the boat incredibly stiff," said Ingate. "It didn't bend when you pulled the runners or the backstay on hard. The International Dragon Class Association 'grandfathered' (accepted as built) this and other rule infractions with the proviso that no more hulls were to be made."

INGATE'S PROGRESS THROUGH the Dragon class results was measured, but improved with age; his age. With Taranui he finished sixth in the 1996 Prince Philip Cup Australian championship, won by

Nick Rogers, ten times Prince Philip Cup winner, in his 1996 win with Karabos VIII, Sydney Harbour / BOB ROSS

Tasmanian Nick Rogers' Karabos VIII, on Sydney Harbour. The following year, in Hobart, Taranui was seventh while local Jock Robbie (Bruce Calvert) won; 1998, at Royal Brighton YC, Taranui fourth, Kirribilli II (Dave Graney, Tasmania) won; 1999, Royal Freshwater Bay YC, Taranui ninth, Isis (Iain MacDiarmid, NSW), won; 2000, Royal Sydney YS, Taranui fifth, Imagination (John Wilson, NSW) won; 2001, Royal Brighton YC, Taranui seventh, Jock Robbie (Nick Chapman, Victoria) won; 2002, Royal Freshwater Bay YC, Taranui ninth. Glenn Tucker, a newcomer the class and a previous Etchells national champion, crewed by Edgar Vitte and Morris Levitzke, won in a new boat, named 188, from the highly-regarded British Dragon builder Petticrow, delivered only ten days before the regatta.

Ingate bought that boat and took delivery straight after the 2003 Dragon world championship and Prince Philip Cup in Hobart where local skipper Nick Rogers, steering Karabos VIII, won his seventh Prince Philip Cup Australian championship preceding the worlds. Germany's Chrisco (Dieter Schoen), a two-year-old Petticrow, won the world championship by a clear 28.3 points from Karabos VIII with another Tasmanian boat Kirribilli II (David Graney), third.

WITH HIS PETTICROW, renamed Whim, Ingate quickly climbed the result sheets. On Sydney Harbour in 2004, crewed by Neville Wittey and Geoff Morris, he finished fifth in the Prince Philip Cup, won by Nick Rogers steering Hugh Wardrop's new Ridgeway-built Leander in a fleet of 20 boats from all states in variable weather from moderate sea breezes to drifters. Leander ended the seven-race series on equal points with Carl Ryves' Sidewinder. The tie was broken in favour of Leander, which had scored three wins to Sidewinder's two. Third was Imagination (Ian MacDiarmid), another three points behind.

Ingate, busy with campaigning a 5.5 for the world championship on Sydney Harbour, did not contest the 2005 and 2006 Prince Philip Cups. With Whim, in 2007 at the Royal Freshwater Bay YC Ingate, crewed by Mark Dorling and Bobby Wilmot, finished fifth in the Prince Philip Cup, in a fleet of 26, sailed in strong winds on the first two days. Puff (Richard Lynn, WA) won from Snapdragon (Andrew Foulkes, WA) with Maalee (Hank Koelemij, WA) third. Whim won the Martin Graney match-racing series and the Ted Albert Memorial regatta, with two wins and a third, preceding the Australian championship.

Whim, winner 2008 Prince Philip Cup on the River Derwent
RICHARD BENNETT

IN 2008, AT the age of 82, Ingate with Whim, crewed by Tasmanians Nick Rogers and Simon Burrows, won the Prince Philip Cup conducted by the Royal Yacht Club of Tasmania on the River Derwent, with 19.7 points, from Riga (Ian McCrossin, NSW) and Kirribilli II (Andrew Crisp, Tasmania), both on 24.7 points. "I decided to take the boat down to Hobart solely based on once I got there I would see if I could get a Tasmanian crew to race with me," said Ingate. "I was confident I would."

Always close, 2008 Prince Philip Cup / RICHARD BENNETT

On arrival at the Royal Yacht Club of Tasmania and inquiring about crew, Ingate was advised to contact Simon Burrows, Nick Rogers' former for'ard hand, who had taken a break from sailing while his wife had a baby.

"He said, 'I am available'.

"I said, 'Isn't Nick sailing in the Prince Philip Cup?'

"'No, because he's got a new boat and it's not ready.'

"So, I gave Nick a call. 'How about crewing for me?'

"'No way, Gordon. I have decided that I am not going to do the Prince Philip Cup this year.'

"'Come on.'

"'Right, on one condition, I'm the tactician.'

"'Of course, Nick. You have done so well in the Prince Philip Cup. I am happy just to sit and steer.'

"We went out for a couple of practice sails, with Rogers on mainsheet and Burrows forward and I was perfectly happy with the way they were handling the boat.

"We get to the starting line of the first race, in a nor'-wester on the River Derwent and I told Nick, 'I will do exactly what you say.'

"Nick said, 'I want you to start right at the starter's boat and tack onto port once you can clear the anchor chain and go all the way to the northern shore. We'll get a lift over there, lay up to the first buoy and we will do extremely well.'

Prince Philip Cup winners 2008, from left: Nick Rogers, Gordon Ingate, Simon Burrows / INGATE FAMILY ARCHIVE

"We got a reasonable start at the starter's boat, weren't pushed out or anything although I thought the best end of the line was the pin end. So, we tacked, cleared the chain and away we went on a long port tack. I happened to look over my shoulder and saw that every other boat was on starboard tack going up towards the bridge, because that's where the mark was and I thought, 'Jesus, they are doing all right over there.'

"The gap became incredibly wide and I thought we should be tacking and going with them.

"And Nick was saying, 'It's okay Gordon, when we tack we are going to lift right up to the mark.'

"I thought, 'Jesus Christ, they're a long way in front.'

"And Nick said, 'Okay, tack now.'

"The moment we tacked, we got the most incredible knock of all times; instead of lifting up to the mark we were getting knocked away from it. We went around the first mark probably three or four minutes behind the last boat.

"And Nick said, 'Gordon, I will never tell you where to go in this series again. You go where you want to go.'

"The next races we got good starts, picked the shifts and in one of the races, which I thought was our best effort, was in a sou'-easter, coming up the river. It was very, very, shifty. I remember in one of the shifts we tacked, went probably two boat lengths, got a helluva knock, tacked again on it and we went half a dozen boat lengths on port, tacked onto starboard, went about six boat lengths; tacked onto port with hardly any way on at all and we gained probably five minutes on the rest of the fleet and we won that race by an awesome margin (3min 45sec).

"Nick said, 'You picked that one right Gordon.'

"But it was a sheer bloody fluke; I tacked because the headsail went aback so hard we had tacked before we had any way on at all.

"We won that Prince Philip Cup mainly because of the ability of Nick and Simon Burrows. Nick Rogers was an outstanding skipper who won ten Prince Philip Cups including the one with me. I was confident, I had a very good crew, the boat was sailing well, I had very good sails and we won. It finally boiled down us doing well in the last race and not getting beaten by the boat that was coming second Riga, skippered by Ian McCrossin. It blew like the clappers; 40 knots by 11 o'clock when we were supposed to go out to the start and the committee, thank heavens, decided to keep us ashore until the breeze dropped. The sailing instructions said that if racing was not possible by two o'clock in the afternoon the race would be cancelled. At two o'clock it was still blowing 30 knots and they declared us the winners. I immediately opened a bottle of port."

Final placings and points (under the old IYRU scoring system): 1, Whim (Gordon Ingate), 9-2-4-1-2-3-abn, 19.70; 2, Riga (Ian McCrossin), 1-6-1-6-5-2-abn, 24.70; 3, Kirribilli II (Andrew Crisp), 4-4-3-2-1-8-abn, 24.70; 4, Leander (Hugh Wardop), 6-1-7-18-7-1-abn, 37.70.

Nick Rogers won his tenth Prince Philip Cup with Karabos IX in January 2009 on Sydney Harbour, by 2.3 points from Ingate's Whim, after a final race duel. Ingate steered Whim into third place while Karabos

Whimsical has the inside overlap, 2012 Prince Philip Cup
ROYAL BRIGHTON YC

IX finished fifth to secure the series win. Russian entry Murka (Olga White) won the race from Ingate's former boat Taranui (Matt Whitnall) with Whim only another 14 seconds behind. If Whim had finished second, Ingate would have retained the Prince Philip Cup by 0.4 of a point. Rogers said: "My objective was to try to drive Gordon back down the fleet, as he had to finish first or second to win. But I let him get by and then had to chase him all the way and keep within a couple of places. Matt Whitnall just beat him across the line for second place and that meant we were the winners."

Whim was third in the 2010 Prince Philip Cup, at Royal Freshwater Bay YC, Perth in a fleet of 29 boats. Local skipper Richard Lynn, with a scorecard of 1-1-4-4-4-2-3 (24.7 points), won from Russian Murka II (Olga White) 3-8-5-3-1-1-4 (29.4) while Whim recorded 12-7-1-1-11-5-2 {43}.

British crew Lawrie Smith, Tim Tavinor and Ossie Stewart, sailing Alfie, won the 2011 world championship at Royal Brighton YC, Melbourne. Their solitary win in race one was enough to give them the title on a placings countback from Bunker Queen (Marcus Weiser, Sweden). Third was My Way (Frank Berg, Denmark), which also won the Corinthian Trophy for the first amateur crew. Scoundrel (Willy Packer,

Whimsical heads up wind in a typical Port Phillip sou'-wester, 2012 Prince Philip Cup / ROYAL BRIGHTON YC

Royal Freshwater Bay YC) was the first Australian boat, in eighth place. Seventy boats competed including 30 in the Corinthian division. The Prince Philip Cup, preceding the worlds, was won by African Queen (Jørgen Schoenher, Denmark). First Australian crew was Richard Lynn, Ian Olsen and Ron Rosenberg, sailing Puff-eu in fourth place. Whimsical, with Gordon Ingate crewed by David Giles and Dan Burrows, placed 45th in the worlds and 22nd in the Prince Philip Cup.

Ingate did not contest the 2012, Prince Philip Cup at the Royal YC of Tasmania. Karabos XI (Nick Rogers/Leigh Behrens/Simon Burrows) won with a loss of seven points, from Indulgence (Robert Campbell) and Shapes (Wolf Breit), both on 23 points, with the tie broken in Indulgence's favour. In 2013 Gordon Ingate's new Petticrow Dragon Whimsical finished second, with 35.0 points, behind Matt Whitnall's Akula, on 17.4 points, in the first Prince Philip Cup to be sailed on Botany Bay, which on the second day had demanding north-west winds of up to 20 knots with 25-knot gusts and temperatures reaching 42.5 degrees. Third was Sidewinder (Carl Ryves, NSW), on 35.4.

Whimsical, crewed by Ingate, David Giles and Brad Sheridan, was third overall in the 2014 Prince Philip Cup, in a fleet of 26, at Royal

Freshwater Bay YC, Racing was very close with five different winners in the seven races. Local Willy Packer, crewed by Julian Harding and Denis Cullity on Scoundrel, sailed a consistent series to come from behind and win the Prince Philip Cup by two points from British based Rob Campbell's Linnea, with Whimsical third another four points behind. Whimsical won the last race. She was in phase with the oscillating breeze, took the lead on the second beat of the three-round windward-leeward course and extended on every leg. Whimsical was the only boat to register two wins in the seven-race regatta.

WHIMSICAL WON THE 2015 Prince Philip Cup, with Ingate crewed by Brad Sheridan and David Giles, by a point at Royal Brighton Yacht Club from British Dragon sailor Robert Campbell sailing the borrowed Sydney boat Indulgence. Third was Shapes (Wolf Breit). All three were from the Royal Sydney Yacht Squadron. The fleet of 16 included boats from Victoria, New South Wales, Tasmania, Western Australia and Great Britain. Ingate began the regatta with 4-3 results on day one then on the second day took the lead with 2-1 ahead of Shapes.

The major opposition came from Breit and Robert Campbell, a past president of the International Dragon Class Association, who until the discard race came into effect on the last day had been carrying a 17-point penalty from an OCS premature start in race two. Campbell, from the Royal Corinthian Yacht Club, UK, a regular visitor to Australia for the Prince Philip Cup, had already made a clean sweep of the Albert Memorial Cup, a precursor to the Prince Philip Cup. Campbell and his crew, Sydney sailors Robert Alpe and Richard Franklin, fought back on day two with a first and a third in races three and four. Racing was abandoned on day three because of extremely stormy weather over Melbourne.

On the final day, with worst race discarded, Indulgence and Whimsical were both on six points behind Shapes on five. The racing started in pouring rain and light wind. Whimsical won race five from Shapes and Indulgence with the scores then being Whimsical and Shapes each on seven points and Indulgence, nine points. Indulgence won the sixth (final) race but Whimsical's second place ahead of Shapes gave Ingate his second Prince Philip Cup. Final scores were: Whimsical 4-3-2-1-1-2, 9 points; Indulgence, 2-OCS-1-3-3-1, 10 points; Shapes, 1-1-3-6-2-3, 10 points.

"By the end of the series it was down to the three boats and Rob was sailing really well," said David Giles. "In the last race at the first top mark we were pretty close together and then on the next beat we just kept pushing Shapes back to the left and taking the shifts to the right in a typical south-west sea breeze; most of the races were sailed in those conditions. We had good starts generally, speed was good. Rob was really challenging because he was going quick in the breeze but we changed a couple of things and we were going better by the end of the series. We won a couple of races and that put us right back into it."

New South Wales champions, 2015, from left: Roger Hickman, Gordon Ingate, David Giles
ROYAL SYDNEY YS

Ingate added: "We changed the settings. We didn't alter the position of the mast but David helped a lot on trimming the genoa for the lumpy Port Phillip sea. Basically, we went for sail power; filled the genoa up like a ballooner of the old 16-footers and I was sailing a bit freer, but faster; not as high as I usually sail on Sydney Harbour, which is flatter and where the advantage I have over the other guys is I just sail high. The reason Wolf Breit did so well with Shapes was he had Roger Hickman on board. I lined Roger up to sail the 2016 Prince Philip Cup with me; he had grown up sailing in Hobart and he believed he could beat Nick Rogers on the Derwent."

SADLY, HICKMAN, WHO was a keen Dragon sailor as well as being an outstanding offshore racer with three Sydney-Hobart race wins to his credit, became severely ill on completing the 2015 Rolex Sydney-Hobart race and was unable to sail with Ingate in the Prince Philip Cup that followed. David Britain, who had been Ingate's forward hand on Gretel II, took his place. Hickman had sailed with Ingate and David Giles in winning the 2015 NSW Dragon class championship in November. "He was excellent to sail with, just excellent," said Ingate. "With David doing the forward hand work, which is extremely important on Dragons, Roger trimmed the mainsheet and called tactics and we just walked away with the state championship."

Whimsical heads the charge into Bradley's head, 2017
Prince Philip Cup race five / BOB ROSS

Ingate, in Hobart preparing for the Prince Philip Cup, visited Hickman at his apartment the day he finished the Hobart race on his Wild Rose and immediately realised Hickman was sick as well as being extremely tired from his four days at sea. "We called an ambulance, got him into hospital and they put him on airplane and sent him to Sydney that afternoon. Dr Teo at North Shore Hospital neurology department found he had this bloody great cyst on his brain. He lived for about six weeks and that was it; a shocker when you look at his history in sailing and what he did for other people involved in sailing."

Nick Rogers, Leigh Behrens and Simon Burrows (forward hand) sailing Karabos IX won the 2016 Prince Philip Cup conducted by the Royal Yacht Club of Tasmania convincingly from Whimsical. Sandra ('Sandy') Anderson was third, also winning the women's title, skippering Linnea. Final placings and points: 1, Karabos IX, 1-3-1-1-2-2-1, 8 points; 2, Whimsical, 2-2-3-2-4-3-3, 15 points; 3, Linnea, 4-1-2-3-1-5-10, 16 points.

Perfect boat and sail trim, Whimsical, 2017 Prince Philip Cup race five
BOB ROSS

NINETY-YEAR-OLD INGATE WON the Prince Philip Cup for the third time in 2017 in a series that came down to the last race on Sydney Harbour. With long-time crew member David Giles working the foredeck and Giles' 22-year-old stepdaughter Aimee Walsh in the middle, Ingate's Whimsical won the deciding last race by 35 seconds from Linnea (Sandy Anderson), from Freshwater Bay YC, Perth. Whimsical won the series with a score line of 14-3-1-6-1-3-4-1 placings for 19 points from Linnea (1-7-6-3-2-20-1-2), 22 points. Third in the fleet of 19 was Robert Campbell's Indulgence from Royal Sydney Yacht Squadron on 27 points. Whimsical began the series with an OCS premature start in race one and so had to sail conservatively, especially in the starts, for the rest of the series.

Whimsical established a huge lead on the first run, race five, 2017 Prince Philip Cup / BOB ROSS

The title eventually came down to the last race between three contenders. Whimsical's crew had to get one boat between them and Indulgence to take the title and Linnea had to finish three ahead of Whimsical and four ahead of Indulgence. Whimsical won by 25 seconds from Linnea. Indulgence was disqualified for a premature start.

Ingate admitted that loss of upper body strength made it difficult for him to steer downwind under spinnaker in winds of more than 20 knots. The last race was sailed in fresh 18-20 knot nor'easter that gusted to 25 knots. "I am really washed out," he said afterwards. He praised David Giles for his tactical ability, agility and great strength. "I couldn't have done it without David, he was fantastic, and I couldn't have done it without his step daughter, who he is training. From a very conservative start in the last race, David picked the wind shifts upwind and was able to keep us in the middle of the best of the incoming tide downwind."

David Giles is a big guy but as agile as a ballet dancer around the foredeck. His skills as a tactician were developed through sailing with Colin Beashel in the Star class at every Olympic regatta from Barcelona 1992 to Athens in 2004 with their best result a bronze medal at Savannah in 1996. The pair were world champions in the Stars in 1998 and with Richard Uechtritz, the Etchells world champions in 1993 and 1995. Giles and Ingate knew their way around Sydney Harbour from years of experience. "We basically tried to sail harbour stuff; smarter in wind and current," said Giles, "And Gordon did a fantastic job keeping his end of the boat under control. Positioning the boat for the shifts comes from big-fleet racing. I don't swing for the corners; I try to chip away inside."

Aimee had sailed with Gordon and David for the first time on Gordon's 88th birthday, March 29, 2014, in a Royal Sydney Yacht Squadron Yngling mini-regatta. "I took her out the afternoon beforehand and showed her how to handle the spinnaker and then we had a three-race series in a howling southerly and won all three races. Aimee is great," said Giles.

Perfect sail trim on Whimsical, pacing a trawler in
the Sydney Harbour traffic / BOB ROSS

"Gordon is one of the best drivers I have sailed with," said Giles. He has a much better touch than other good helmsmen I have sailed with; he is world class and he is fantastic in light air. We have worked together for a long time and developed modes of sailing. He knows how to get the best out of a Dragon; he has great feel and knows when to sail in high mode or low mode. I can always rely on him to be accurate with his helming, which helps with our tactics. If you ask him to quickly tack for a certain position, he is quite capable of doing that. It is obviously harder for him to get around the boat as he has got older but the helming skills have not gone down. I have sailed with him 12 years and he

At the 2017 Prince Philip Cup, Royal Sydney YS presentation, from left, David Giles, Gordon Ingate, Aimee Walsh / ROYAL SYDNEY YS

is sailing better now than he did then. Physically, he says he doesn't like sailing downwind in over 20 knots of wind. Dragons are tough to steer downwind in high winds with the rudder hanging off the long, the big fat keel. And Gordon thinks about the big picture. The downfall of a lot of people is to think about the one boat they are up against, not the three or more boats. Gordon is much better with the big picture."

WHILE REMAINING EXTREMELY competitive on the Australian scene, each winter Ingate would head to the northern hemisphere with his partner Margaret Hearder to sail, socialise and sightsee in Europe in the Dragon and 5.5 classes and the USA for the annual New York Yacht Club cruise, until Margaret died in 2015. Among the overseas regattas he attended in the Dragons were:

- 2004 chartered Yankee Doodle Dandy from Glen Foster for the Dragon Gold Cup at Falmouth, finished 25th in a fleet of 40. Get-a-way (Frank Berg, Denmark) won.

- 2006 Kiel Week, crewed by David Giles and Brian Faith, 21st with Yankee Doodle Dandy in a fleet of 35. They also sailed in the Dragon Grand Prix, Kiel before the 5.5 world championship at Aarhus in Denmark.
- 2011: British East Coast championship Burnham on Crouch, Edinburgh Cup: 23rd in chartered Whimsey, 43 starters.
- 2012: Dragon Gold Cup, Kinsale YC, Ireland. Edinburgh Cup, Belfast
- 2013 Dragon worlds, Weymouth chartered Clairvoyant, crewed by David Giles and Dayne Sharp, 55th in a fleet of 77.
- 2015 Dragon Worlds, La Rochelle, France, Little Hook crewed by David Giles and Brad Sheridan, 41st in a fleet of 80. Winner Bunker Boys (Yevgen Braslivets, UAE).

IN MARCH 2019, Ingate made Whimsical available to the Royal Sydney Yacht Squadron crew, skippered by Matt Whitnall with David Giles and David Chapman, which narrowly won the historic Sayonara Cup in a match-racing series on the Derwent River, Hobart, from the Royal Yacht Club of Tasmania defender Karabos IX skippered by Nick Rogers with crew Leigh Behrens and Oliver Burnell.

The Sayonara Cup contest was created as an interstate challenge between Australian Royal Clubs in 1904, first contested by 80ft gaff-rigged cutters, the Royal Yacht Club of Victoria's Sayonara (Alfred Gollin) and Bona (Herbert Binnie), representing the Royal Sydney Yacht Squadron.

Sayonara sailed from Melbourne to Sydney and won the best two of three race contest off Sydney Heads. Gollin then presented the ornate silver cup as a trophy in perpetuity for interstate challenge matches.

For the next 58 years, the Sayonara Cup became Australia's leading big boat match-racing contest, eventually in Eight Metre class yachts. With the focus on big-boat match racing moving to the Australian America's Cup challenges in Twelve Metres, interest in the Sayonara Cup then lapsed until the 1980s when it resumed in International Dragon class one-designs and changed trophy cabinets between the Royal Sydney Yacht Squadron, Sydney's Royal Prince Edward YC and the Royal Yacht Club of Tasmania.

After Karabos IX, skippered by Nick Rogers, regained the trophy from the Royal Sydney YS in 2009, it sat unchallenged in the RYCT until 2019 when the RSYS issued a challenge inspired by member Nicole Shrimpton, owner of the Eight Metre Defiance, who saw the magnificent trophy at the

Whimsical leads Karabos IX in a mark rounding / PENNY CONACHER / RYCT

RYCT while visiting Hobart to see the finish of the Sydney-Hobart race.

She persuaded the Squadron to enter a challenge for 2019 and her friend Gordon Ingate to become patron of the challenge and provide his Whimsical for Whitnall, Chapman and Giles to sail against Rogers' Karabos IX.

Ingate, about to turn 93, was happy to stand down for the younger skipper but enjoyed steering Whimsical on the River Derwent the day before the contest.

Whimsical (AUS 217) won the race three after a gybing duel / PENNY CONACHER / RYCT

Although the RSYS won 4-2, the racing was extremely close. In the six races the winning margin was only once greater than 14 seconds; in race three just one second separated the two boats as they finished; in race five two seconds. In race three, Whimsical made three fast spinnaker gybes just before the finish to gain right of way over Karabos IX and cross one second ahead.

"The Sayonara Cup was the most exciting match racing I have ever seen," said Ingate. "The excitement of the racing was unbelievable. We already have a challenge from Royal Freshwater Bay YC. They want to challenge in Dragons."

Ingate organised the transport of Whimsical to and from Hobart with his friend and crewmate David Giles doing the driving as well as sailing in the crew. Giles who is large, besides being extremely fit, had to lose 19 kilos in 14 days for Whimsical's crew to weigh in under the limit of 285kg for three crew.

At the Cup presentation, from left: Gordon Ingate, David Giles, Matt Whitnall, David Chapman, Nicolle Shrimpton
PENNY CONNACHER / RYCT

"He went without food for 14 days and was riding his bike 50 kilometres a day. I don't know how that bloke is still alive. He drove the trailer from the farm to Sydney, to Melbourne, boarded the ferry to Launceston, drove to Hobart and rigged the boat up by himself. Then he made the return journey to the Squadron and put the mast back in. He is fantastic; he does the lot."

SADLY, 62 YEARS of Dragon class club racing in Sydney came to an end in the 2017-18 season when insufficient entries were received. Royal Sydney Yacht Squadron had to shuffle the boats entered – Whimsical, Intrigue (Gavin Moss) and Abracadabra (Nicholas Hogg and John Marty) into the number three division mixed fleet. "It is just terrible," said Ingate.

However, Dragon racing passion was restored for Ingate in January 2018, when in a strong fleet of 25 boats Ingate, again crewed by David Giles and Aimee Walsh sailing Whimsical, won the Prince Philip Cup for the fourth time on the Gippsland Lakes in Victoria, from Robert Campbell's Pennyfarthing.

Final points and placings for the leaders: 1, Whimsical (G.Ingate, Royal Sydney YS), 6-1-1-3-9-1-2, 14; 2, Pennyfarthing (R.Campbell,

Royal Corithian YC), 1-4-5-1-7-3-4, 18; 3, Adios III (Grant Aldersea, Metung YC), 3-2-4-4-11-8-3, 24.

The series was sailed in strong south-westerly winds that raised a difficult chop on the shallow waters of Lake King. And the competitors had to sail an hour and a quarter from the Metung Yacht Club near the entrance to the Lakes to reach the course. "I was getting to the stage where I was tired before we got to the start line and thought 'Jesus, this is going to be hard.'"

In the deciding last race, approaching the windward mark for the first rounding on the windward-leeward course, Pennyfarthing was leading and Whimsical was fifth. Pennyfarthing needed to finish at least two places ahead of Whimsical to win the series.

"As I came around on starboard tack, bearing away to a reaching course as we had done in the previous races, with Ghost (Johno Johnson) right behind me. I was hearing his bow wave and suddenly I wasn't hearing it. They were still hard on the wind."

"I thought they were withdrawing from the race. However, I noticed that the stick mark (clearing offset mark on the windward-leeward course) was in position but there had been a dramatic change of course because the first windward mark had drifted downwind by 50 metres or so.

"I came hard on the wind and had to pinch like buggery to get to the clearing mark. The others had gone around where they thought it was and all had to tack back to get around it and were overtaken by the balance of the fleet.

"We went around second to Ghost but she was leading comfortably because we had to pinch to lay the mark and were going slow. We couldn't make any impression for the rest of the race against Ghost, a 30-year-old boat, well-sailed by a young crew.

"But that second won us the Prince Philip Cup; not good tactical sailing by Gordon but sheer arse, as in the saying 'Every time I bend over a rainbow pops out from my arse', put around about ten years ago by my friend Bill Manning.

"When you think of it, my life span to date has been rainbows. I haven't had any major illnesses; I haven't had any bad financial problems, I have done reasonably well in my sailing career and from that point of view the rainbows and arses fit very well."

THE AWARDS

MOST SIGNIFICANT AMONG THE TREASURED awards Gordon Ingate has received is a Medal of the Order of Australia (OAM) in the General Division for services to sailing in the 2016 Queen's Birthday honours list.

The sport's governing body, Australian Sailing, commenting on the announcement, said: "Gordon has had an enormously long sailing history, both in Australia and internationally, having sailed for more than 75 years and has proudly represented his country in some of the most prestigious international events.

"Governor of the Sydney Heritage Fleet since 2000 and long-time member of the Royal Sydney Yacht Squadron, Cruising Yacht Club of Australia, New York Yacht Club and past member of the Sydney Amateur Sailing Club, he is still an active and competitive sailor."

Australian Sailing president Matt Allen added: "Gordon has had a huge influence over many decades and classes and is well respected for his efforts at home and internationally, including the Admiral's Cup, America's Cup and Olympic Games.

"He is a great character and personality in the sport, well known across the world and as he recently celebrated his 90th birthday and is still winning and competing; he's an inspiration for all of us and truly signifies this is a sport for life."

In June 2019, Ingate received the Royal Sydney Yacht Squadron's Life Achievement Award, given at the discretion of the Commodore (David Ward) at the annual prizegiving if there was an outstanding achievement to be recognised.

RSYS Club Captain Karyn Gojnich said: "Gordon is living proof that sailing is a sport for life. He has had such a rich and diverse sailing career. If we all managed to do half of what Gordon has done and still be sailing in our nineties, we will be very fortunate."

Ingate untypically struggled to find words to reflect on the awards and his life in general. But he found them expressed in the lyrics of his favourite Frank Sinatra song "I did it my way".

"I've lived a life that's full
I've travelled each and every highway
But more, much more than this,
I did it my way."

Gordon added: "Ingate did it his way with self-belief and the passion for sailing which is like nothing else. It has over-ridden my married life, my family life and my business life. I always put the other things to one side.

"It makes me a pretty selfish sort of a guy.

"I did it my way."

Bob Ross footnote:
Gordon Ingate is not selfish. He has touched the lives of many people, with special concern for his friends and family, as well as his cheerful and sociable nature.

www.ingramcontent.com/pod-product-compliance
Lightning Source LLC
Chambersburg PA
CBHW071231080526
44587CB00013BA/1563